FAITH FADING

How Christianity is Disappearing from Schools, Government and Corporate America

MYLES MCGUIRE

CONTENTS

INTRODUCTION

In a small classroom somewhere in America, a teacher once asked a group of students to name the founding principles of their country. A hand shot up, and a young voice confidently declared, "Freedom, justice, and God." The room fell silent, and the visibly uncomfortable teacher gently corrected the student, steering the discussion toward secular principles. This moment, though seemingly trivial, underscores a profound shift in our society. The mention of God, once integral to our nation's ethos, now evokes hesitation and discomfort.

"Faith Fading: How Christianity is Disappearing from Schools, Government, and Corporate America" seeks to explore this shift. Why has our society, which once proudly proclaimed its faith, begun to distance itself from Christianity? What are the implications of this detachment for our moral and spiritual fabric?

The thesis of this book is clear: as schools, government, and corporate America move away from Christian principles, the moral and spiritual integrity of our society weakens. This is not merely a lament for a bygone era but a call to understand the consequences of this transformation.

I am a person of faith, raised in the Catholic tradition. My formative years were spent in Catholic schools, including post-graduate executive business studies at the University of Notre Dame. My journey has always been intertwined with faith, leading me to explore various perspectives on Christianity and beyond. Conversations with individuals from different religious backgrounds, particularly those with varying views on Christianity, have enriched my understanding. Despite minor differences, the core values of Christianity remain consistent. Given this, I grapple with why institutions today are distancing themselves from these principles.

My motivation for writing this book stems from a deep concern for the future of our society. As a father who has continued the tradition of sending his child to Catholic school and as a senior executive who has witnessed the erosion of faith-based principles in Fortune 500 companies, I feel compelled to address this issue. This book is a reflection of my lived experiences, academic background, and professional observations.

Historically, Christianity has played a pivotal role in shaping Western civilization. Our founding documents, such as the Declaration of Independence, reference God and the divine rights of individuals. Our currency bears the inscription, "In God We Trust." These references are not mere historical artifacts but symbols of the foundational values that have guided our nation. Yet, in contemporary times, there is an unmistakable trend towards secularization. Schools avoid religious discussions, government policies increasingly sideline faith-based considerations, and corporate America prioritizes profit over principles.

The scope of this book includes an exploration of the historical context, an analysis of the current state of faith in various institutions, and a discussion of the potential future. We will examine the role of Christianity in schools, the government, and corporate America, delving into how and why these institutions have shifted their stance.

The book is organized into chapters, each focusing on a specific aspect of this shift. The first chapter provides a historical overview, tracing the roots of Christianity in America. The subsequent chapters explore the current state of faith in schools, government, and corporate America, supported by case studies and statistical data. The final chapters discuss the implications of this shift and propose potential pathways for re-integrating faith into our societal framework.

By the end of this book, I hope readers will gain a deeper understanding of the significance of faith in our societal structures. This is not a call for a theocracy but a plea for balance. Recognizing and respecting the role of Christianity in our history and present can provide moral and ethical guidance in an increasingly complex world.

I encourage you to reflect on your own experiences and observations. How has the shift away from faith impacted your life? What values do you hold dear, and how are they reflected in the institutions you interact with? This book is an invitation to engage in a critical dialogue about the role of faith in modern society.

Let us embark on this journey together, exploring the past, understanding the present, and envisioning a future where faith and reason coexist harmoniously. The stakes are high, but the potential for positive change is immense.

THE HISTORICAL FOUNDATIONS OF FAITH IN AMERICA

A brisk wind swept across the steps of Independence Hall as Thomas Jefferson dipped his quill into ink, preparing to inscribe the words that would echo through the annals of history. It was not merely a declaration of political autonomy, but a proclamation imbued with an acknowledgment of divine authority. As Jefferson penned the Declaration of Independence, he introduced a framework that would intertwine faith and governance, a legacy that would shape the nascent nation. This chapter explores the profound influence of Christianity on America's founding documents, examining how religious references and Christian morality were deeply embedded in the nation's foundational texts.

THE ROLE OF CHRISTIANITY IN THE FOUNDING DOCUMENTS

The Declaration of Independence, a seminal document that laid the groundwork for American democracy, is replete with references to a higher power. Terms such as "Nature's God" and "Creator" are not merely rhetorical flourishes but deliberate invocations of a divine authority that legitimizes the rights and freedoms delineated within the text. The phrase "Laws of Nature and of Nature's God" acknowledges a cosmic order presided over by a divine entity, suggesting that human laws must align with this higher moral framework. Similarly, the assertion that all men are "endowed by their Creator with certain unalienable Rights" positions God as the ultimate guarantor of human dignity and freedom.

The Enlightenment era, during which the Declaration was conceived, was characterized by a burgeoning emphasis on reason and scientific inquiry. Yet, many Enlightenment thinkers, including key figures among the Founding Fathers, were theists who believed in a rational deity. This belief in a god who established natural laws influenced their conception of governance and rights. Biblical references in the Declaration, such as the assertion of "unalienable Rights" endowed by the Creator, echo the scriptural notion of inherent human dignity. These references underscore the belief that rights are not granted by governments but are intrinsic to human nature, a concept rooted in Christian theology.

Christian morality also played a pivotal role in shaping early American laws. The moral imperatives derived from biblical teachings provided a framework for justice and governance. The influence of Christian ethics is evident in the early legal codes that emphasized fairness, justice, and the protection of individual rights. These principles, drawn from biblical injunctions, laid the foundation for a legal system that sought to balance individual freedoms with communal responsibilities.

Prominent Christian figures among the Founding Fathers further reinforced the integration of faith and governance. John Witherspoon, a clergyman and a signer of the Declaration, was instrumental in shaping the moral and intellectual underpinnings of the document. His sermons and writings emphasized the importance of virtue and piety in public life, advocating for a government that reflected Christian values. Benjamin Franklin, though often remembered for his pragmatic and secular contributions, proposed the idea of opening the Constitutional Convention with prayer. This proposal, though not adopted, reflected his belief in the necessity of divine guidance in the nation's most critical endeavors.

John Adams, another key figure, frequently corresponded on matters of faith and governance. In his letters, Adams articulated the view that religion and morality were indispensable supports for political prosperity. He believed that a republic could only thrive if its citizens were virtuous and moral, a belief deeply rooted in his Christian faith. These convictions influenced the framing of the Constitution and the establishment of a government that sought to promote the common good while safeguarding individual liberties.

The Northwest Ordinance of 1787, another critical document in American history, explicitly recognized the role of religion in governance and education. The ordinance declared that "religion, morality, and knowledge being necessary to good government and the happiness of mankind, schools and the means of education shall forever be encouraged." This provision underscored the belief that a well-educated populace, grounded in moral and religious principles, was essential for the success of the Republic. The ordinance also provided for land grants to support religious education, demonstrating a commitment to integrating faith into the fabric of societal development.

The public and private writings of the Founding Fathers further illuminate their views on religion and its role in governance. In his Farewell Address, George Washington emphasized the importance of religion and morality as "indispensable supports" for political prosperity. He warned against the notion that morality could be maintained without religion, underscoring the belief that faith was integral to the nation's well-being. In his letters, Thomas Jefferson often discussed the role of religion in government, advocating for religious freedom while recognizing the moral foundation that faith provided.

The historical foundations of faith in America are deeply entwined with the nation's founding documents and the beliefs of its early leaders. Christianity provided a moral and intellectual framework that shaped the principles of governance and justice, influencing the development of a society that valued individual rights and communal responsibilities. As we examine these foundational influences, it becomes clear that the legacy of faith is not a relic of the past but a vital thread in the fabric of American identity.

FAITH AND GOVERNANCE IN EARLY AMERICA

In the nascent stages of American governance, the integration of Christian principles was not merely incidental but foundational. Early American laws were profoundly influenced by biblical teachings, as evidenced by the proliferation of "blue laws" which mandated moral conduct in accordance with Christian doctrine. These laws, originating in the 17th century, prohibited various activities on Sundays, reflecting the biblical commandment to keep the Sabbath holy. They were not mere legal formalities but deeply rooted in the communal conscience, aiming to cultivate a society that revered divine statutes.

Blasphemy laws, which criminalized irreverence towards God, and laws against Sabbath-breaking were common in colonial legal codes, underscoring the moral imperatives derived from Scripture. These statutes were designed to maintain public order and piety, reflecting a societal consensus that moral decay was inimical to the common good. Early legal codes, such as the Massachusetts Body of Liberties of 1641, explicitly incorporated biblical injunctions, setting a precedent for a legal system that sought to align human law with divine will. The moral foundations of these laws were not abstract ideals but practical guidelines for living a life that honored God and community.

Church leaders were pivotal in the political life of early America, wielding influence that extended beyond the pulpit. The "Black Robe Regiment," a term coined by the British, referred to the patriot pastors who played a crucial role during the Revolutionary War. These clergymen, wearing their black clerical robes, preached sermons that galvanized the colonists to fight for liberty, framing the struggle for independence as a divine mandate. Their involvement was not limited to spiritual exhortation; many took up arms and served as chaplains, embodying the belief that faith and freedom were inextricably linked.

The participation of clergy in town meetings and local governance further illustrates their integral role in shaping early American politics. Ministers often presided over civic gatherings, offering prayers and moral guidance that influenced legislative decisions. Their sermons, delivered from the pulpit, were not confined to theological discourse but addressed pressing social and political issues, providing a moral framework for public policy. This symbiotic relationship between church and state was evident in the multifunctional use of church buildings, which served as venues for town meetings and community events. Churches were not just places of worship but community centers where civic and spiritual life converged.

As community leaders and moral guides, ministers were central figures in early American society. Their influence extended beyond religious instruction to encompass a broad range of social and political activities. They were often consulted on matters of public concern and played a key role in mediating disputes, reflecting the high regard in which they were held. This integration of faith and civic life created a cohesive community where moral and spiritual values informed governance.

The religious rhetoric in early presidential addresses further underscores the integration of faith and governance. In his first inaugural address, George Washington invoked divine guidance, expressing his reliance on "the benign parent of the human race" for wisdom in leading the nation. His acknowledgment of a higher power set a precedent for future leaders, emphasizing the importance of faith in political life. In his inaugural address, John Adams referred to divine providence, underscoring his belief in a God who actively guided the affairs of nations. These references were not perfunctory but reflected a deeply held conviction that the success of the American experiment depended on divine favor.

In early America, the integration of Christian principles in laws and governance was a testament to the profound influence of faith on the nation's development. This chapter has explored how biblical teachings shaped legal codes, the pivotal role of church leaders in political life, the symbiotic relationship between church and state, and the religious rhetoric in early presidential addresses. These elements collectively illustrate the foundational role of Christianity in shaping the moral and political landscape of early America.

THE INFLUENCE OF RELIGION ON EARLY AMERICAN EDUCATION

In the early days of American history, education was not merely an academic endeavor but a moral and spiritual undertaking deeply intertwined with religious instruction. The founding of religiously affiliated colleges and universities stands as a testament to the profound influence of Christianity on education. Harvard University, established in 1636, was founded primarily to train clergy for the burgeoning Puritan colony. Its mission was clear: to ensure that future generations would be educated leaders who could read and interpret the Scriptures. This commitment to religious education was not unique to Harvard but was echoed in the establishment of other institutions. Yale University, founded in 1701, also operated under a religious charter that emphasized the importance of training ministers and upholding Christian values. Similarly, Princeton University, established in 1746, had its roots in Presbyterianism and aimed to educate students in both secular knowledge and religious doctrine. These institutions were not merely centers of learning but bastions of faith dedicated to preserving and perpetuating Christian teachings.

Early American schools were permeated with religious instruction, and the curriculum was designed to foster both intellectual and spiritual growth. The New England Primer, widely used in colonial schools, combined literacy education with religious teachings. This small book, with its alphabet lessons interwoven with biblical references, was a staple in early American education. Students learned their ABCs alongside catechisms and moral lessons, ensuring that their literacy was grounded in a Christian worldview. Daily prayers and Bible readings were integral parts of the school day, reinforcing the notion that education was a divine endeavor. Religious texts were not confined to theology classes but were used across subjects to teach literacy and moral values. The Bible, regarded as the ultimate source of wisdom and knowledge, was frequently used to teach reading, writing, and ethical conduct. This approach ensured that students' academic development was inextricably linked to their spiritual formation.

Religious societies played a significant role in promoting education, recognizing that an educated populace was essential for both spiritual and civic life. The American Bible Society, founded in 1816, was instrumental in distributing Bibles across the nation, ensuring that individuals had access to the Word of God. Their efforts were not limited to adults but extended to children, with the aim of inculcating biblical values from a young age. The Sunday School movement, which began in the late 18th century, had a profound impact on literacy and religious education. These schools, often run by local churches, provided basic education to children who might otherwise have had no access to schooling. They taught reading and writing through the lens of biblical stories and principles, fostering both academic and spiritual growth. The movement's emphasis on education for all children, regardless of social class, reflected a deep commitment to the teachings of Christ, who welcomed and valued every individual.

The legal and social support for religious education was robust, with colonial laws often mandating religious instruction and community norms strongly encouraging it. Many colonies enacted laws requiring that children receive a religious education, recognizing the importance of instilling Christian values in the young. For example, the Massachusetts School Laws of 1642 and 1647 mandated that parents and guardians ensure their children could read and understand the principles of religion and the laws of the colony. These laws underscored the belief that education was not merely a private matter but a public good, essential for maintaining a moral and orderly society. Parochial schools, supported by local communities, played a crucial role in this educational landscape. These schools, often affiliated with specific churches, provided a more rigorous religious education than public schools, emphasizing doctrinal instruction and moral formation. Community support for these institutions was strong, with parents and local leaders recognizing the value of a faith-based education in cultivating virtuous citizens.

Early American education was deeply intertwined with religious instruction, reflecting a societal consensus that faith and learning were mutually reinforcing. The founding of religiously affiliated colleges and universities, the curriculum of early schools, the efforts of religious societies, and the legal and social support for religious education all highlight the profound influence of Christianity on the development of American education. This integration of faith and learning not only shaped the intellectual landscape of the early Republic but also laid the foundation for a society that valued both spiritual and academic growth.

CHRISTIANITY IN EARLY AMERICAN COMMERCE

The integration of Christian ethics into early American commerce was not merely an incidental occurrence but a deliberate endeavor to align business practices with biblical principles. Usury, or the charging of exorbitant interest on loans, was explicitly prohibited, reflecting the biblical injunction against exploiting the vulnerable. This prohibition was rooted in passages such as Exodus 22:25, which admonished against lending money to the poor at interest. Early American businesses adhered to this principle, ensuring that financial transactions were conducted fairly and ethically, safeguarding the welfare of individuals and communities alike.

Fair weights and measures were another cornerstone of commerce guided by biblical teachings. Leviticus 19:35-36 commands, "You shall have just balances, just weights," underscoring the importance of honesty in trade. This biblical mandate was not only a moral directive but a practical one, fostering trust and integrity in commercial transactions. Businesses that adhered to these standards were seen as reputable and trustworthy, creating a marketplace where fairness and justice prevailed. This adherence to ethical practices was not merely a reflection of personal piety but a societal expectation deeply ingrained in the fabric of early American commerce.

Philanthropy and charitable giving were also integral to business practices, driven by the Christian imperative to care for the less fortunate. The teachings of Jesus, particularly the parable of the Good Samaritan, inspired people in business to view their wealth as a means to serve others. This ethos of generosity was manifest in the establishment of hospitals, schools, and other charitable institutions funded by Christian businessmen. These acts of philanthropy were not seen as optional but as a moral obligation, reflecting the belief that wealth should be used for the common good.

Religious groups played a significant role in economic development, contributing to commerce in ways that extended beyond individual business practices. Quaker businesses, for instance, were renowned for their ethical practices, earning a reputation for fairness and integrity. The Quaker's commitment to honesty and simplicity was evident in their business dealings, fostering a culture of trust and reliability. This ethical approach to commerce not only garnered respect but also proved to be economically advantageous, as consumers preferred to engage with businesses that upheld these moral standards.

The Puritan work ethic, grounded in the belief that hard work was a form of worship, had a profound economic impact. This ethos, encapsulated in the phrase "idle hands are the devil's workshop," encouraged diligence and industriousness. Puritans viewed their labor as a calling from God, imbuing their work with a sense of purpose and meaning. This commitment to hard work and productivity contributed significantly to the economic development of early American society, fostering a culture of diligence and perseverance.

Christian philanthropy had a lasting influence on early American society, with businesses actively supporting religious and social causes. The establishment of charitable organizations like the YMCA was driven by Christian businessmen who sought to address social issues through faith-based initiatives. These organizations provided essential services, such as housing and education, to marginalized communities, reflecting the Christian mandate to "love thy neighbor." The funding of hospitals and schools by Christian businessmen further exemplified this commitment to social welfare, ensuring that the benefits of economic prosperity were shared with those in need.

The motivations behind early American entrepreneurship were often deeply rooted in religious convictions. A prominent businessman, John Wanamaker seamlessly integrated his faith with his business practices. He viewed his department stores not merely as commercial enterprises but as extensions of his Christian mission, providing fair wages and fostering a supportive work environment. Another notable figure, Henry Heinz, was similarly motivated by his faith, emphasizing honesty and quality in his food production business. He famously declared that his company would "do a common thing uncommonly well," reflecting his belief that ethical practices were integral to business success.

In early American commerce, Christian ethics were not peripheral but central, guiding business practices and fostering a culture of integrity and generosity. The contributions of religious groups to economic development, the influence of Christian philanthropy, and the motivations of business leaders driven by faith collectively illustrate the profound impact of Christianity on the commercial landscape of early America. This integration of faith and commerce created a marketplace where ethical practices were not only valued but expected, shaping the moral and economic trajectory of the nation.

THE EVOLUTION OF RELIGIOUS FREEDOM

The trajectory of religious freedom in America from its colonial inception to the ratification of the Bill of Rights reveals a complex interplay of legal, social, and theological influences. The Maryland Toleration Act of 1649, often heralded as a pioneering statute for religious liberty, mandated tolerance for Trinitarian Christians within the colony. This Act, enacted by the Maryland Assembly, was a significant step towards legal protection for religious diversity. It was a pragmatic response to sectarian conflicts and aimed to create a more harmonious society by ensuring that Catholics and Protestants could coexist under the law. Although the Act was later repealed, its legacy endured, setting a precedent for the legal recognition of religious pluralism.

The Virginia Statute for Religious Freedom, drafted by Thomas Jefferson in 1777 and enacted in 1786, marked a monumental shift towards the separation of church and state. Jefferson's statute asserted that religious belief was a matter of personal conscience and that civil rights should not be contingent upon religious adherence. This seminal document not only disestablished the Church of

England in Virginia but also laid the philosophical groundwork for the First Amendment. Jefferson's powerful declaration, "No man shall be compelled to frequent or support any religious worship, place, or ministry whatsoever," encapsulated the emerging American ethos of religious liberty and would later influence the drafting of the Bill of Rights.

The First Amendment to the United States Constitution ratified in 1791, enshrined religious freedom as a fundamental right, prohibiting Congress from making any law "respecting an establishment of religion, or prohibiting the free exercise thereof." These twin clauses—the Establishment Clause and the Free Exercise Clause—were designed to ensure that the government neither favored nor inhibited religious practice. This constitutional guarantee was a response to the diverse religious landscape of the new nation and reflected a commitment to protecting individual conscience against governmental interference.

Dissenting religious groups, such as Baptists and Quakers, played pivotal roles in advocating for religious freedom. The Baptists, particularly in Virginia, were staunch advocates for the disestablishment of state-supported churches, arguing that true faith could not be coerced. Their persistent lobbying and influential writings were instrumental in shaping public opinion and legislative action toward greater religious liberty. Similarly, the Quakers, with their emphasis on inner light and personal revelation, passionately pushed for tolerance and the protection of individual religious conscience. Their commitment to pacifism and social justice further underscored the moral imperative for a society that respected religious diversity.

Landmark legal cases have continually shaped the contours of religious freedom in America. In Reynolds v. United States (1879), the Supreme Court tackled the issue of polygamy, ruling that while religious beliefs are inviolable, practices that contradict social order and morality could be regulated. This case established the precedent that the Free Exercise Clause does not protect actions that violate criminal laws. In Cantwell v. Connecticut (1940), the Court affirmed the right to free exercise of religion, ruling that states could not unduly burden religious practices through restrictive licensing laws. This decision underscored the principle that religious expression is a fundamental liberty deserving robust protection. Engel v. Vitale (1962), which struck down state-sponsored prayer in public schools, further delineated the boundaries of the Establishment Clause, emphasizing the need to maintain a secular public sphere free from governmental endorsement of religion.

Societal and cultural shifts have significantly influenced the understanding and application of religious liberty over time. The Great Awakening, a series of religious revivals in the 18th century, fostered an environment of religious pluralism and fervor that challenged established ecclesiastical hierarchies and promoted individual spiritual experience. This movement democratized religious practice, paving the way for a more inclusive conception of religious freedom. Immigration has also played a crucial role in diversifying America's religious landscape. Waves of immigrants brought with them a plethora of faith traditions, enriching the nation's spiritual tapestry and necessitating legal frameworks that accommodated this diversity.

The evolution of religious freedom in America is a testament to the nation's enduring commitment to individual conscience and the protection of spiritual autonomy. From the early legislative efforts to enshrine tolerance through the robust advocacy of dissenting groups to the landmark judicial decisions that have continually redefined the boundaries of religious liberty, America's journey toward religious freedom reflects a dynamic interplay of legal, social, and cultural forces. This rich tapestry of historical milestones and legal precedents underscores the importance of vigilance in safeguarding the delicate balance between the free exercise of religion and the secular nature of the state.

As we reflect on this complex history, it becomes evident that the principles of religious freedom are not static but must be continually interpreted and defended in light of changing societal contexts. The legacy of these foundational efforts to protect religious liberty remains a cornerstone of American identity, reminding us of the profound importance of allowing every individual the freedom to believe, worship, and practice their faith without fear of persecution or coercion.

THE DECLINE OF CHRISTIANITY IN MODERN EDUCATION

Picture a bustling 19th-century classroom where children, seated on wooden benches, recited passages from the Bible as part of their daily lessons. This scene, once emblematic of American education, has dramatically transformed over the centuries. The gradual secularization of public schools is a narrative of profound change driven by a series of pivotal events and ideological shifts.

SECULARIZATION OF PUBLIC SCHOOLS: A HISTORICAL OVERVIEW

The establishment of the "common school" movement in the 19th century marked a significant departure from the religiously infused education of earlier times. Spearheaded by Horace Mann, often hailed as the "father of American education," this movement aimed to provide universal education accessible to all children, irrespective of their socio-economic background. Mann's vision was revolutionary, advocating for a non-sectarian education system that excluded specific religious instruction. His belief was that education should serve as a democratic equalizer, preventing rigid class systems and supporting the nascent democracy in the United States (Source 1).

Mann's efforts were instrumental in laying the groundwork for the modern interpretation of the separation of church and state. He argued that while schools should inculcate moral values based on universal Christian principles, they should not act as arbiters between competing religious doctrines. This non-sectarian approach faced significant opposition, particularly from Roman Catholic leaders who perceived it as embodying general Protestant principles. Nevertheless, Mann's vision prevailed, setting a precedent for future educational policies and court rulings that would further entrench secularism in public education.

The rise of the "separation of church and state" doctrine gained further momentum through a series of landmark legal battles. One of the most significant cases in this trajectory was McCollum v. Board of Education (1948). This case revolved around the practice of "released time," where public schools set aside class time for religious instruction by outside religious teachers. Vashti McCollum, an atheist, challenged this practice, arguing that it violated the Establishment Clause of the First Amendment and the Equal Protection Clause of the Fourteenth Amendment. The Supreme Court, in an 8-1 decision, ruled in her favor, asserting that the use of tax-supported property for religious instruction and the close cooperation between school authorities and religious councils violated the constitutionally mandated separation of church and state (Source 2).

Another pivotal case was Abington School District v. Schempp (1963), which challenged the practice of mandatory Bible readings in public schools. The Supreme Court ruled that such practices were unconstitutional, reinforcing the principle that public schools should remain secular spaces free from religious endorsement. This ruling, alongside others, gradually eroded the presence of religious activities in public education, further entrenching the separation of church and state.

The Lemon v. Kurtzman (1971) case introduced the "Lemon Test," a three-pronged standard for determining violations of the Establishment Clause. This test required that any government action must have a secular legislative purpose, must not advance or inhibit religion, and must not result in excessive government entanglement with religion. The Lemon Test became a critical tool in subsequent rulings, providing a clear framework for evaluating the constitutionality of religious activities in public institutions. These legal precedents collectively shaped the secularization of public education, ensuring that religious instruction and activities were systematically removed from public schools.

The influence of secular humanism in education further accelerated this shift. John Dewey, a prominent philosopher and educator, championed the philosophy of pragmatism, which emphasized experiential learning and critical thinking over rote memorization and dogmatic instruction. Dewey's vision for education was inherently secular, advocating for a curriculum that focused on humanist principles and empirical science. His ideas profoundly impacted American education, shifting the focus from religious teachings to a more secular, student-centered approach (Source 3).

Secular ideologies gradually replaced religious teachings in school curricula, emphasizing moral and ethical development through a humanist lens. Character education programs, which focused on virtues such as honesty, respect, and responsibility, were introduced to instill moral values without religious connotations. These programs aimed to promote ethical behavior and social-emotional learning, fostering a sense of civic responsibility and community engagement among students.

Educational policies played a crucial role in promoting secularization. Policies mandating the removal of religious symbols from classrooms and the establishment of guidelines for secular holiday observances were implemented to ensure that public schools remained neutral spaces. These policies aimed to create an inclusive environment that respected the diverse religious beliefs of students and their families, adhering to the principle of separation of church and state.

The secularization of public schools represents a significant transformation in American education, driven by historical movements, legal battles, and ideological shifts. The establishment of the "common school" movement, the rise of the separation of church and state doctrine, and the influence of secular humanism collectively contributed to the removal of religious elements from public education. As we reflect on these changes, it becomes evident that the secularization of education has fundamentally altered the moral and spiritual landscape of American society.

THE REMOVAL OF PRAYER AND BIBLE READING FROM SCHOOLS

The legal and cultural shifts leading to the removal of prayer and Bible reading from American public schools represent a significant transformation in the educational landscape. The landmark case Engel v. Vitale (1962) serves as a pivotal moment in this narrative. The Supreme Court ruled that state-sponsored prayer in public schools, even if non-denominational and voluntary, violated the Establishment Clause of the First Amendment. This decision was a watershed moment, signaling a decisive move towards secularization in public education. The case arose from a New York State law requiring public schools to begin each day with the Pledge of Allegiance and a non-denominational prayer. Parents, alarmed by the state's endorsement of religious activity, challenged the law, arguing it constituted an unconstitutional government intrusion into religious matters (Source 4).

The ruling generated a wave of cultural backlash and ignited fervent public debates. Many saw the decision as an affront to the nation's religious heritage, fearing it would erode the moral fabric of society. Letters to editors, public demonstrations, and heated discussions in community forums reflected a nation grappling with the implications of this judicial decree. For some, it was a necessary step to uphold the constitutional principle of separation of church and state; for others, it was a stark departure from the moral and spiritual underpinnings that had long defined American public life.

The removal of prayer and Bible reading had profound implications for school culture. Morning routines and assemblies, once punctuated by communal prayers and scriptural readings, underwent significant changes. The practice of beginning the school day with a moment of collective spiritual reflection was replaced by secular activities such as reciting the Pledge of Allegiance or observing a moment of silence. This shift not only altered the rhythm of daily school life but also transformed the nature of classroom discussions and moral teachings. Teachers, who had previously incorporated biblical lessons into their instruction, now turned to secular texts and humanist principles to impart moral values. The focus moved from a shared religious framework to a more inclusive, yet often morally ambiguous, approach.

Advocacy groups played crucial roles in both supporting and opposing the removal of religious practices from schools. The

American Civil Liberties Union (ACLU) emerged as a prominent advocate for the separation of church and state, launching campaigns to challenge religious activities in public institutions. Their efforts were instrumental in bringing cases like Engel v. Vitale to the courts, arguing that government endorsement of religion infringed upon individual freedoms and violated constitutional principles. Conversely, religious groups mobilized to oppose these rulings, asserting that removing prayer and Bible readings would strip schools of their moral foundation. These groups organized rallies, lobbied legislators, and initiated legal challenges, striving to maintain a place for faith in public education.

The long-term effects of these changes on students and communities are multifaceted. For students, the removal of prayer and Bible reading has had significant implications for their moral and spiritual development. In the absence of religious instruction, students often turn to secular sources for moral guidance, which may lack the coherent ethical framework provided by religious teachings. This shift has led to concerns about the moral relativism and ethical ambiguity that can arise in a secular educational environment. Communities, too, have had to adapt to these changes, grappling with the loss of a unifying spiritual practice that once fostered a sense of shared values and communal identity.

In response, some communities have sought to reintroduce elements of faith through private religious education or after-school programs, while others have embraced the secular model, focusing on inclusivity and diversity. The debate over the role of religion in public schools continues to evoke strong emotions and divergent opinions, reflecting the ongoing tension between maintaining a secular public sphere and acknowledging the spiritual heritage that has shaped the nation.

THE SHIFT FROM RELIGIOUS TO SECULAR MORAL EDUCATION

The evolution from religious to secular moral education reflects a profound shift in the philosophical underpinnings and pedagogical approaches within American schools. Character education programs emerged as a direct response to the increasing secularization of public education, seeking to instill core ethical values without invoking religious doctrine. These programs emphasize virtues such as respect, responsibility, and integrity, aiming to foster moral development in a manner that is inclusive of all students, regardless of their religious backgrounds. The introduction of character education marked a significant departure from the explicitly religious moral teachings that had previously dominated American classrooms.

Parallel to the rise of character education, social-emotional learning (SEL) curricula began to take root in the educational landscape. SEL programs focus on developing students' emotional intelligence, self-awareness, and interpersonal skills, promoting a holistic approach to moral education. These curricula are grounded in psychological theories and aim to equip students with the tools to navigate complex social dynamics, manage their emotions, and make responsible decisions. The development of SEL reflects a broader trend towards integrating cognitive and emotional aspects of learning, recognizing that moral development is inextricably linked to emotional well-being.

The philosophical underpinnings of secular moral education are diverse, drawing from various ideological traditions. Utilitarianism, with its emphasis on the greatest good for the greatest number, has significantly influenced these programs. This ethical framework prioritizes outcomes and consequences, encouraging students to consider the broader impact of their actions on society. Utilitarian principles are often embedded in character education programs, guiding students to make decisions that promote collective well-being and minimize harm.

Existentialist thought, which emphasizes individual autonomy and the creation of personal meaning, has also shaped secular moral education. Existentialism challenges students to take responsibility for their actions and to construct their own moral frameworks independent of external authorities. This philosophical perspective aligns with the goals of SEL, which encourages students to reflect on their values and develop a sense of purpose and identity. By fostering critical thinking and self-reflection, existentialist principles help students navigate moral dilemmas and make ethical choices in a complex, pluralistic world.

The content and implementation of secular moral education vary widely, but successful programs share certain commonalities. Character education programs often incorporate a mix of direct instruction, experiential learning, and reflective activities. For example, programs may include lessons on ethical decision-making, opportunities for community service, and discussions on real-life moral dilemmas. These activities aim to engage students actively and to reinforce moral principles through practical application. Case studies of successful character education programs reveal that a multifaceted approach, combining theoretical knowledge with experiential learning, is most effective in promoting moral development.

Social-emotional learning activities are designed to cultivate emotional intelligence and interpersonal skills. These activities may include role-playing scenarios, mindfulness exercises, and collaborative projects. The objectives of SEL activities are to help students develop empathy, manage stress, and build positive relationships. By integrating these activities into the daily curriculum, schools aim to create a supportive and inclusive environment that fosters both academic and personal growth.

Despite the potential benefits of secular moral education, these programs are not without their criticisms and challenges. Religious communities often argue that secular moral education lacks a coherent ethical framework and fails to provide the moral absolutes that religious teachings offer. They contend that without a transcendent source of morality, secular programs may lead to moral relativism, where ethical standards are fluid and subjective. This criticism highlights a fundamental tension between secular and religious approaches to moral education, reflecting broader societal debates about the role of religion in public life.

Measuring the effectiveness of secular moral education presents another significant challenge. Unlike academic subjects, moral development is inherently subjective and difficult to quantify. Educators and researchers grapple with questions about how to assess students' moral growth and how to determine the long-term impact of these programs. While some studies suggest that character education and SEL can positively influence students' behavior and academic performance, definitive conclusions are elusive. The complexity of moral development and the diversity of educational contexts make it challenging to evaluate these programs' success comprehensively.

The shift from religious to secular moral education represents a significant transformation in the way schools approach moral development. As you reflect on these changes, consider how they have impacted the educational experiences of students and the ethical landscape of our society.

FAITH-BASED SCHOOLS VS. PUBLIC SCHOOLS: A COMPARATIVE ANALYSIS

Walking through the hallways of a faith-based school, you might observe classrooms where religious studies are seamlessly integrated into the curriculum. These institutions often place a strong emphasis on teaching biblical principles alongside traditional subjects. In a history class, for example, students might examine the impact of religion on the development of Western civilization, drawing connections between historical events and theological shifts. Religious studies are not mere adjuncts but core components of the educational experience, fostering an environment where faith and learning coexist harmoniously.

In contrast, public schools adhere to a secular curriculum without religious instruction. Subjects such as history, science, and literature are taught through a strictly secular lens, ensuring compliance with the principle of separation of church and state. While moral and ethical discussions may arise, they are framed within a secular context, drawing from a variety of philosophical traditions rather than religious doctrines. This approach aims to create an inclusive environment that respects the diverse beliefs of all students, yet it often lacks the cohesive moral framework provided by religious teachings.

The moral and ethical teachings in faith-based schools are deeply rooted in biblical principles. Students are encouraged to cultivate virtues such as honesty, compassion, and humility, drawing inspiration from the teachings of Christ. Moral education in these settings is explicit and intentional, with Scripture serving as the foundation for ethical instruction. Students might participate in chapel services, engage in community service projects, and study religious texts, all of which reinforce a moral code grounded in faith.

In public schools, moral education is framed within secular moral frameworks. Character education programs and social-emotional learning (SEL) curricula aim to instill values such as respect, responsibility, and empathy. These programs draw from various philosophical traditions, including humanism and utilitarianism, to promote ethical behavior. However, without the anchoring presence of religious doctrine, the moral guidance provided can sometimes appear fragmented or inconsistent. The emphasis is on fostering ethical reasoning and social skills, but the absence of a transcendent moral authority can lead to ethical relativism.

When examining the academic performance and social outcomes of students from faith-based and public schools, the data reveals intriguing patterns. Studies have shown that students in faith-based schools often outperform their public school counterparts in standardized tests and college admission rates. The disciplined environment and emphasis on moral character contribute to a culture of academic excellence. Additionally, faith-based schools foster strong social behaviors and community involvement. Students are often engaged in service projects and extracurricular activities that promote a sense of civic responsibility and altruism.

In public schools, academic performance can vary widely, influenced by factors such as socio-economic status, funding, and community support. While many public schools achieve high academic standards, others struggle with limited resources and challenging environments. Social behavior and community involvement also vary, with some schools fostering strong student engagement and others facing issues such as bullying and low participation in extracurricular activities. The absence of a unified moral framework can sometimes hinder efforts to cultivate a cohesive and supportive school culture.

Community and parental involvement play crucial roles in the success of both faith-based and public schools, yet they manifest differently in each setting. In faith-based schools, community support systems are often robust, with parents, teachers, and religious leaders working together to create a nurturing environment. Parental involvement is typically high, reflecting a shared commitment to the school's mission and values. Parents may participate in school events, volunteer for activities, and engage in regular communication with teachers and administrators.

In public schools, parental involvement can vary significantly. While some parents are highly engaged, participating in parent-teacher associations and school events, others may have limited involvement due to work commitments or other factors. Public schools often strive to build strong community ties, offering programs and initiatives to encourage parental engagement. However, the absence of a shared religious framework can make it more challenging to foster a cohesive community spirit.

Faith-based schools and public schools offer distinct educational experiences, each with its own strengths and challenges. The inclusion of religious studies, moral teachings based on biblical principles, and strong community support systems in faith-based schools create an environment where academic excellence and moral development are intertwined. In contrast, public schools, with their secular curricula and diverse student populations, aim to provide an inclusive education that respects individual beliefs while promoting ethical behavior through secular frameworks. This comparative analysis underscores the complex interplay between education, morality, and community, highlighting the unique contributions and limitations of each educational model.

THE IMPACT OF SECULAR EDUCATION ON MORAL DEVELOPMENT

Theories of moral development have significantly influenced secular education, providing a framework for understanding how individuals evolve in their ethical reasoning. Lawrence Kohlberg's stages of moral development offer a comprehensive model for this progression. Kohlberg proposed that moral reasoning matures through a series of stages, beginning with a pre-conventional level where decisions are based on avoiding punishment and seeking rewards. As individuals progress, they reach the conventional level, where societal norms and the desire for social approval guide behavior. Ultimately, some attain the post-conventional level, where abstract principles and the recognition of universal ethical principles govern decisions. This model has been instrumental in shaping educational strategies that emphasize moral reasoning and ethical decision-making.

In her critique of Kohlberg, Carol Gilligan introduced the ethics of care, which focuses on relationships and empathy rather than abstract principles. Gilligan argued that traditional models of moral development, including Kohlberg's, often overlooked the importance of care and compassion, especially in how women approach ethical dilemmas. Her theory posits that moral development involves a deepening understanding of the interconnectedness of individuals and the responsibilities that arise from these relationships. This perspective has enriched secular moral education by emphasizing the role of empathy, nurturing, and relational ethics.

The practical implications of these theories in secular moral education are profound. Educators implement moral reasoning activities designed to challenge students to think critically about ethical dilemmas. These activities often involve case studies that present complex moral situations, requiring students to navigate conflicting values and perspectives. For instance, a classroom might analyze a scenario where a student must choose between loyalty to a friend and honesty about a friend's wrongdoing. Through guided discussions and reflective exercises, students explore the nuances of moral decision-making, learning to balance personal integrity with social responsibilities.

Case studies of moral dilemmas are frequently used to illustrate the application of these theories. For example, a case study might involve a business leader faced with the decision to cut costs by laying off employees or finding alternative solutions that might be less profitable but more ethical. Students analyze the situation, considering the implications of each choice and the underlying moral principles. This approach enhances critical thinking and fosters a deeper understanding of the complexities inherent in ethical decision-making.

The broader societal outcomes of secular moral education reveal significant shifts in norms and values. As secular education emphasizes critical thinking and ethical reasoning, societal attitudes toward morality have evolved. There is a growing acceptance of diverse perspectives and a recognition of the importance of empathy and compassion in ethical considerations. This shift is evident in the increasing emphasis on social justice, environmental stewardship, and human rights, all of which reflect a more inclusive and nuanced understanding of morality.

However, the correlation between secular education and social behavior is complex and multifaceted. While secular moral education has succeeded in promoting critical thinking and ethical awareness, it has also faced challenges in providing a cohesive moral framework. Critics argue that without a transcendent source of morality, secular education can lead to moral relativism, where ethical standards are fluid and subjective. This concern is particularly pronounced among religious communities, who contend that secular moral education lacks the definitive moral absolutes provided by religious teachings.

Support for secular moral education comes from various quarters, including secular organizations and educators who advocate for a pluralistic approach to morality. They argue that secular education fosters an inclusive environment that respects diverse beliefs and promotes ethical reasoning based on universal principles of justice and compassion. Proponents highlight the benefits of teaching students to navigate moral dilemmas independently, using critical thinking and empathy rather than relying on external authorities.

The debate over secular moral education reflects broader societal tensions between religious and secular worldviews. While secular education has made significant strides in promoting ethical reasoning and empathy, it continues to grapple with the challenge of providing a coherent and universally accepted moral framework. These ongoing debates underscore the complexity of moral education in a pluralistic society, highlighting the need for continued dialogue and reflection on how best to cultivate ethical individuals.

In examining the impact of secular education on moral development, it becomes clear that this shift has brought both opportunities and challenges. The application of moral development theories, the implementation of moral reasoning activities, and the broader societal outcomes all reveal a nuanced picture of how secular moral education shapes individuals and communities. As we navigate these complexities, it is essential to consider the diverse perspectives and values that inform our understanding of morality and ethical behavior.

CHRISTIANITY AND GOVERNMENT

A Gradual Separation

Imagine, if you will, a time when the words spoken by the President of the United States were imbued with the solemn reverence of a Sunday sermon. This was the America of George Washington and Abraham Lincoln, where religious rhetoric was not merely a ceremonial flourish but a cornerstone of political discourse. Washington's Farewell Address, delivered in 1796, is a prime example of this integration. In his valedictory speech, Washington emphasized the indispensable role of religion and morality in the prosperity of the nation, asserting that "religion and morality are indispensable supports" for political prosperity. His invocation of divine providence was not a mere formality but a reflection of his deep-seated belief that the Republic's success was inextricably linked to the favor of Almighty God.

The Civil War era further underscored the intertwining of faith and politics. Abraham Lincoln's Second Inaugural Address, delivered in 1865, stands as a testament to the power of religious rhetoric in a time of national crisis. Grappling with the moral and existential weight of the Civil War, Lincoln framed the conflict in theological terms, interpreting the war as a divine judgment upon the nation for the sin of slavery. He famously stated, "The Almighty has His own purposes," suggesting that the war was a manifestation of God's will. This speech, suffused with biblical references and theological reflections, offered solace and a moral framework to a nation ravaged by conflict, underscoring the belief that divine justice and mercy were integral to the American ethos.

However, the landscape of political rhetoric has undergone a profound transformation since those early days. The Enlightenment, with its emphasis on reason, empiricism, and secularism, laid the groundwork for a gradual shift towards more secular language in political discourse. Enlightenment thinkers championed the separation of church and state, arguing that governance should be based on rational principles rather than religious dogma. This intellectual movement fostered a culture of skepticism towards religious authority, paving the way for a more secular approach to political rhetoric.

The rise of pluralism in the modern era further necessitated a shift towards inclusive language. As America became increasingly diverse, with a multitude of religious and non-religious perspectives coexisting, political leaders began to adopt a more secular tone to appeal to a broader audience. The need to respect and represent this diversity led to a deliberate avoidance of overtly religious rhetoric, which could alienate significant portions of the electorate. This shift was not merely a pragmatic decision but a reflection of the evolving social contract, which sought to balance respect for individual beliefs with the principles of democratic inclusivity.

Media and public opinion have played crucial roles in shaping this transformation. The advent of television and social media has amplified the reach and impact of political rhetoric, subjecting it to unprecedented levels of scrutiny and instant public reaction. Political speeches are now dissected, analyzed, and debated in real-time, with every word and gesture scrutinized for its potential impact. This heightened visibility has made political leaders more cautious in their use of religious language, aware that any perceived favoritism or exclusion could spark controversy and backlash.

Television, in particular, has been instrumental in shaping political discourse. The visual medium demands brevity and clarity, often eschewing the nuanced and reflective language that characterized earlier speeches. The need for sound bites and media-friendly quotes has led to a simplification of political rhetoric, stripping it of the rich theological and philosophical undertones that once defined it. Social media has further accelerated this trend, with platforms like Twitter favoring succinct and direct communication over-elaborate and contemplative expressions.

Public reactions to overtly religious speeches have also influenced this shift. While some segments of the population resonate deeply with religious rhetoric, others perceive it as exclusionary or inappropriate in a pluralistic society. This polarization has led political leaders to tread carefully, striving to strike a balance between acknowledging the nation's religious heritage and respecting its secular principles. The delicate task of appealing to a diverse electorate has necessitated a cautious approach to religious language, often resulting in a more neutral and inclusive tone.

The implications of this shift for religious communities are significant. Many religious voters feel alienated by the secularization of political rhetoric, perceiving it as a departure from the values they hold dear. This sense of alienation has prompted efforts by religious groups to influence political campaigns, striving to ensure that their voices are heard and their values represented. These efforts often involve lobbying, grassroots mobilization, and strategic alliances with sympathetic political leaders.

However, the relationship between religious groups and politicians has become increasingly complex. While some politicians continue to incorporate religious language to appeal to faith-based constituencies, others adopt a more secular tone to avoid alienating non-religious voters. This balancing act reflects the broader societal tension between maintaining a secular public sphere and acknowledging the enduring influence of religious values. The evolving dynamics of this relationship underscore the ongoing negotiation between faith and politics in a rapidly changing cultural landscape.

THE ROLE OF THE JUDICIARY IN SECULARIZING GOVERNMENT

The judiciary has played a pivotal role in the secularization of American government, with several landmark Supreme Court cases setting the tone for the separation of church and state. One of the earliest and most influential decisions was **Everson v. Board of Education (1947)**. This case centered around a New Jersey law that reimbursed parents for transportation costs to parochial schools. The Supreme Court upheld the law, but in doing so, Justice Hugo Black famously invoked Thomas Jefferson's metaphor of a "wall of separation between church and State." This decision, while allowing for the reimbursements, reinforced the principle that the government should remain neutral in matters of religion, setting a precedent for subsequent rulings.

A significant turning point came with **Engel v. Vitale (1962)**, which addressed the constitutionality of state-sponsored prayer in public schools. The New York State Board of Regents had composed a non-denominational prayer to be recited daily. Parents challenged this practice, arguing it violated the Establishment Clause of the

First Amendment. The Supreme Court agreed, ruling that government-imposed prayers in public schools were unconstitutional. This decision underscored the necessity of maintaining a secular educational environment free from governmental endorsement of religious practices.

The **Lemon v. Kurtzman (1971)** case further solidified the judiciary's stance on secularism by introducing the "Lemon Test," a three-pronged criterion for determining whether a law violates the Establishment Clause. The case involved state laws that provided financial support to religious schools. The Supreme Court ruled these laws unconstitutional, establishing that any government action must have a secular purpose, must not advance or inhibit religion, and must avoid excessive government entanglement with religion. The Lemon Test has since become a critical tool in evaluating the constitutionality of various religious activities in public institutions.

The judicial philosophy behind these decisions is deeply rooted in the interpretation of the Establishment Clause, which prohibits the government from making any law "respecting an establishment of religion." The justices have consistently used historical context and legal precedent to ensure that government actions do not encroach upon religious freedom or favor one religion over another. For instance, in Everson v. Board of Education, the Court's reliance on Jefferson's metaphor highlighted the historical intent behind the First Amendment. By examining the framers' original understanding, the justices aimed to preserve the foundational principle of religious neutrality in government affairs.

Lower courts have also played a crucial role in enforcing secular policies and handling cases that further delineate the boundaries of religious expression in public spaces. Numerous legal battles have addressed the constitutionality of religious displays on public property. For example, in **Lynch v. Donnelly (1984)**, the Supreme Court ruled that a nativity scene displayed in a public park did not violate the Establishment Clause, provided it was part of a broader holiday display that included secular symbols. However, in **County of Allegheny v. ACLU (1989)**, the Court ruled that a nativity scene displayed alone inside a courthouse did violate the Establishment Clause, as it amounted to government endorsement of religion.

Legal battles over religious exemptions and accommodations have further shaped the landscape of religious expression. Cases like **Burwell v. Hobby Lobby Stores, Inc. (2014)**, which allowed for-profit corporations to deny contraceptive coverage based on religious beliefs, highlight the ongoing tension between religious freedom and governmental regulations. These rulings reflect a complex interplay between protecting individual religious rights and maintaining secular governance.

Judicial rulings have profoundly influenced both public and private religious practices. Restrictions on religious activities in public schools, such as the prohibition of school-sponsored prayers and Bible readings, have reinforced the secular nature of public education. These rulings aim to create an inclusive environment where students of all faiths can learn without feeling coerced or marginalized. Similarly, limitations on government funding for religious organizations ensure that taxpayer money is not used to support religious activities, maintaining the separation of church and state.

The judiciary's role in secularizing government underscores the delicate balance between preserving religious freedom and upholding secular principles. By interpreting the Establishment Clause through historical context and legal precedent, the courts have sought to protect individual religious rights while preventing government endorsement of religion. This ongoing judicial oversight ensures that the foundational principle of separation between church and state remains a cornerstone of American democracy.

THE IMPACT OF POLICY CHANGES ON RELIGIOUS EXPRESSION

Over the past century, policy changes have profoundly reshaped the landscape of religious expression in America, often restricting manifestations of faith in public spaces and government institutions. Consider the policies prohibiting religious displays in public areas, such as nativity scenes or menorahs on government property during festive seasons. These regulations, driven by the desire to uphold the separation of church and state, aim to prevent any perception of government endorsement of a particular faith. A notable example is the removal of the Ten Commandments monument from the Alabama Supreme Court building in 2003. This decision, rooted in the Establishment Clause, reflects the growing insistence on maintaining a secular public sphere free from religious symbolism.

Regulations on religious attire and symbols in government institutions further exemplify this trend. Policies that restrict the wearing of religious headscarves, crosses, or other faith symbols by government employees aim to project an image of neutrality and impartiality. These regulations are particularly contentious in countries like France, where the principle of laïcité, or secularism, is stringently enforced. In the United States, while less pervasive, similar debates have emerged, challenging individuals' rights to express their faith openly in public service roles. These policies, while intended to ensure neutrality, often clash with personal freedoms and religious convictions, creating a complex legal and social landscape.

The motivations behind these policy changes are multifaceted and rooted in both social and political imperatives. Efforts to maintain neutrality in a pluralistic society are paramount; in a nation characterized by diverse religious beliefs, the government must tread carefully to avoid appearing biased towards any particular faith. This commitment to neutrality is not merely a legal obligation but a social necessity designed to foster an inclusive environment where all individuals, regardless of their religious beliefs, feel equally represented and respected. However, this drive for impartiality often leads to concerns about religious favoritism and discrimination. Policies aimed at ensuring neutrality can inadvertently marginalize religious communities, particularly when they are perceived as targeting specific faith practices or symbols.

The legal and social challenges to these policies are numerous and often contentious. Religious organizations frequently file lawsuits challenging regulations that they perceive as infringing on their rights to free expression and worship. These lawsuits, which can ascend to the highest courts, are pivotal in shaping the legal interpretations of the First Amendment. Public protests and advocacy campaigns also play crucial roles in opposing restrictive policies. Grassroots movements, supported by religious and civil liberties groups, mobilize to defend the rights of individuals to express their faith openly and without fear of retribution. These campaigns often attract significant media attention, highlighting the ongoing tensions between religious freedom and secular governance.

The broader implications for religious freedom are profound and far-reaching. For religious minorities, policy changes that restrict religious expression can lead to feelings of exclusion and alienation. These communities, already vulnerable to discrimination, may find their rights further eroded by regulations ostensibly designed to promote neutrality. The impact on public attitudes towards religious expression is also significant. As policies increasingly restrict religious displays and symbols, society's perception of faith in public life shifts. Religious expression becomes confined to private spheres, altering the traditional role of faith as a visible and integral part of community life.

This transformation has nuanced repercussions for the exercise of religious rights. On one hand, it reinforces the secular nature of public institutions, ensuring that government remains neutral and inclusive. On the other hand, it challenges individuals' abilities to express their faith openly, raising questions about the balance between secularism and religious freedom. These policy changes, while striving to uphold constitutional principles, often navigate a delicate and contentious path. The evolving landscape of religious expression in America is a testament to the ongoing negotiation between maintaining secular governance and respecting the diverse faith traditions that enrich the nation's cultural fabric.

CHRISTIANITY AND SOCIAL POLICY: PAST AND PRESENT

In the annals of American history, the influence of Christian principles on social policy is both profound and pervasive, shaping the moral and ethical framework of the burgeoning nation. One cannot discuss the history of social reforms without acknowledging the critical role of Christianity in the anti-slavery movement. Abolitionists, many of whom were devout Christians, viewed the institution of slavery as a moral abomination antithetical to the teachings of Christ. Figures like William Lloyd Garrison and Harriet Beecher Stowe invoked biblical principles to argue against the dehumanization inherent in slavery, framing their cause as a divine mandate to uphold the sanctity of human dignity. The moral fervor that characterized the abolitionist movement was deeply rooted in Christian theology, which posited that all men are created in the image of God and thus deserving of equal rights and respect.

Similarly, Christianity played a pivotal role in the establishment of charitable organizations, many of which laid the groundwork for modern social welfare programs. The Salvation Army, founded in the 19th century by William and Catherine Booth, exemplifies this legacy. Driven by a mission to emulate Christ's compassion for the poor and marginalized, the organization provided food, shelter, and spiritual guidance to those in need. These early charitable endeavors were not mere acts of benevolence but were seen as moral imperatives, grounded in the belief that faith without works is dead. This ethos of service and charity, deeply embedded in Christian doctrine, spurred the creation of numerous hospitals, orphanages, and schools, all aimed at uplifting the downtrodden and embodying the teachings of Jesus.

Over time, however, the focus of social policies has shifted, transitioning from religious-based initiatives to secular social programs. This evolution reflects broader societal changes, including the rise of secular humanism and the increasing pluralism of American society. Once profoundly intertwined with religious missions, welfare policies have gradually adopted a more secular framework. For example, the New Deal programs of the 1930s marked a significant departure from faith-based charity, emphasizing government responsibility for social welfare. While still influenced by moral considerations, these programs were framed in secular terms, focusing on economic stability and social security rather than religious duty.

The underlying principles of welfare policies have also evolved, moving from a paternalistic approach to one that emphasizes individual rights and social justice. Early welfare programs often operated under the assumption that recipients needed moral reform as much as material aid, reflecting a Christian ethos of redemption and transformation. In contrast, contemporary social policies prioritize the dignity and autonomy of individuals, advocating for equitable access to resources and opportunities. This shift is evident in policies that address systemic inequalities and promote social inclusion, reflecting a broader commitment to justice and human rights.

Despite these changes, religious organizations continue to play a significant role in modern social policy, often partnering with government agencies to deliver services. Faith-based initiatives, such as those under the Charitable Choice provisions of the Personal Responsibility and Work Opportunity Reconciliation Act of 1996, exemplify this collaboration. These initiatives allow religious organizations to receive government funding for social services, provided they do not use the funds for religious activities. This partnership leverages the strengths of both sectors, combining the resources and oversight of government with the community trust and moral commitment of religious organizations.

However, these collaborations are not without challenges. Legal and regulatory hurdles often complicate the relationship between faith-based organizations and the state. Issues of religious freedom, discrimination, and the separation of church and state frequently arise, necessitating careful navigation to ensure compliance with constitutional principles. For example, controversies over whether faith-based organizations can require employees to adhere to specific religious beliefs or practices highlight the complexities of these partnerships.

Debates over the role of religion in social policy remain contentious. Proponents argue that faith-based organizations bring unique strengths to social services, including deep community ties, holistic approaches to well-being, and a moral commitment to service. They contend that excluding these organizations from government partnerships undermines the effectiveness of social programs and ignores the valuable contributions of religious communities. Critics, however, raise concerns about the potential for religious discrimination and the erosion of the separation of church and state. They argue that government funding for religious organizations risks endorsing specific faiths and infringing on the rights of individuals to receive services free from religious influence.

Discussions on the separation of church and state in social policy are particularly fraught, reflecting broader societal tensions over the role of religion in public life. While the Establishment Clause of the First Amendment prohibits government endorsement of religion, the Free Exercise Clause protects individuals' rights to practice their faith. Balancing these constitutional principles in the context of social policy requires nuanced understanding and careful regulation to ensure that both religious freedom and secular governance are upheld. The current landscape of social policy, shaped by both historical legacies and contemporary debates, underscores the enduring complexities of integrating faith and governance in a pluralistic society.

THE FUTURE OF FAITH IN AMERICAN POLITICS

The landscape of religious affiliation in America is undergoing a seismic shift with significant implications for the political arena. One of the most striking trends is the rise of the "nones," a term used to describe individuals who identify as religiously unaffiliated. According to recent studies, this group now constitutes a substantial portion of the population, particularly among younger generations. This demographic shift suggests a move away from traditional religious institutions and towards a more individualized spirituality or secular worldview. Younger generations, in particular, are increasingly disenchanted with organized religion, often citing hypocrisy, irrelevance, or a preference for scientific rationalism as reasons for their disaffiliation. This trend raises questions about the future role of religion in shaping political values and behaviors.

Religious lobbying and advocacy groups have long played a pivotal role in American politics, wielding considerable influence over legislation and policy. Organizations like the Family Research Council and the Christian Coalition have been instrumental in shaping the political landscape, particularly on issues related to family values, religious freedom, and social conservatism. These groups engage in various activities, from lobbying legislators and mobilizing grassroots campaigns to conducting research and disseminating information to the public. Their impact on legislation is significant, often swaying policy decisions and shaping public opinion on contentious issues such as abortion, same-sex marriage, and religious exemptions. The effectiveness of these organizations underscores the enduring power of religious advocacy in a rapidly secularizing society.

The potential for interfaith coalitions in politics presents both opportunities and challenges. Successful interfaith initiatives, such as the Interfaith Alliance, demonstrate the power of collaborative efforts in advancing shared goals, such as social justice, religious freedom, and community service. These coalitions unite diverse religious groups to work towards common objectives, fostering mutual understanding and respect. However, building and maintaining such coalitions requires navigating theological differences and overcoming historical tensions. The potential areas for future cooperation are vast, ranging from advocacy on climate change and poverty alleviation to promoting peace and conflict resolution. The success of these initiatives depends on the willingness of religious leaders to engage in dialogue and collaboration, recognizing that their shared values can serve as a powerful catalyst for positive change.

The future relationship between religion and government in America can unfold in several ways, each with its own set of implications. One possible scenario is the continued secularization of society, driven by the growing influence of the "nones" and the increasing emphasis on scientific rationalism and individual autonomy. In this context, religious institutions may find themselves increasingly marginalized, with their influence on public policy and political discourse diminishing. This trend could lead to a more pluralistic and inclusive society but also risks eroding the moral and ethical foundations historically provided by religious teachings.

Conversely, a resurgence of religious influence could emerge in response to cultural shifts and societal challenges. Periods of crisis or moral uncertainty often prompt a return to foundational values, with religion serving as a source of solace, guidance, and social cohesion. In such a scenario, religious groups could reassert their influence over political processes, advocating for policies that reflect their moral and ethical convictions. This resurgence could foster a renewed emphasis on community, compassion, and social justice, but it also risks exacerbating tensions between religious and secular worldviews.

The future of faith in American politics is a complex and multifaceted issue, shaped by evolving demographics, the activities of religious advocacy groups, and the potential for interfaith collaboration. As we navigate these changes, it is essential to consider the diverse perspectives and values that inform our understanding of religion's role in public life. The ongoing negotiation between secular and religious influences will continue to shape the moral and political landscape, reflecting the dynamic interplay between tradition and modernity.

As we move into the next chapter, we will explore how these trends in religious affiliation and political influence intersect with broader societal changes, examining the implications for education, governance, and community life. This exploration will provide a deeper understanding of the evolving relationship between faith and public life, highlighting the challenges and opportunities that lie ahead.

CHRISTIANITY'S WANING INFLUENCE IN CORPORATE AMERICA

The boardroom was a solemn place where decisions were made not only for profit but also with a keen awareness of moral imperatives. Early American businesses were often guided by Christian ethics, a framework that infused corporate culture with a sense of divine accountability. This integration of faith and commerce was not merely symbolic but deeply practical. For instance, the prohibition against deceit and misrepresentation was a cornerstone of business ethics, derived directly from biblical injunctions such as Proverbs 11:1, which states, "A false balance is an abomination to the Lord, but a just weight is his delight." This biblical mandate for honesty ensured that transactions were conducted with integrity, fostering trust between businesses and consumers.

Moreover, the fair treatment of workers was a principle rooted in Christian teachings. The Bible, particularly in passages like Colossians 4:1, admonishes masters to provide their servants with what is "just and fair," recognizing that they, too, have a Master in heaven. This directive translated into business practices that emphasized fair wages, humane working conditions, and a general sense of duty towards employees' well-being. Employers who adhered to these principles were seen as not only morally upright but also as fostering a productive and loyal workforce. The emphasis on honesty and integrity in transactions created a business environment where ethical dealings were the norm, and reputational capital was built on a foundation of trustworthiness and reliability.

As we transition to the modern era, the corporate landscape has undergone a significant transformation, moving from a foundation of Christian ethics to a framework dominated by secular principles. One of the primary catalysts for this shift has been the influence of shareholder theory, which prioritizes profit maximization above all else. This theory, articulated by economists like Milton Friedman, posits that the sole responsibility of a corporation is to its shareholders, effectively sidelining broader ethical considerations in favor of financial returns. This profit-centric approach has reshaped corporate priorities, often at the expense of the moral and ethical values that once guided business practices.

The rise of secular humanism has also played a crucial role in redefining business ethics. Secular humanism, with its emphasis on human reason, ethics, and justice, operates independently of religious doctrines. This philosophical shift has permeated corporate culture, promoting a values system based on rationality and empirical evidence rather than divine commandments. While secular humanism advocates for ethical behavior, its principles are often more fluid and adaptable than the fixed moral codes derived from religious teachings. This fluidity can lead to a more flexible approach to ethics, responsive to changing societal norms but potentially less anchored in absolute moral standards.

The divergence between Christian and corporate ethical standards is evident in several key areas. One notable difference is the approach to employee welfare and labor practices. As mentioned earlier, Christian ethics emphasize the fair and humane treatment of workers, viewing them as individuals endowed with intrinsic worth. In contrast, the modern corporate focus on efficiency and cost-cutting can sometimes lead to practices that prioritize productivity over employee well-being. This shift is evident in the rise of precarious employment conditions, such as gig work and zero-hour contracts, which offer flexibility and cost savings for employers but often at the expense of job security and benefits for workers.

Charitable giving and community involvement also illustrate the divergence between these ethical frameworks. Christian business leaders historically viewed philanthropy as a moral obligation, a way to manifest their faith and contribute to the common good. This ethos of generosity was driven by biblical teachings on charity and stewardship. In contrast, modern corporate philanthropy is often strategic, aligned with business objectives and brand image rather than purely altruistic motives. While corporate social responsibility (CSR) initiatives can have significant positive impacts, they may also be driven by considerations of public relations and market positioning rather than a genuine commitment to ethical principles.

The impact of this ethical shift on corporate behavior is profound and multifaceted. One of the most significant consequences is the increased focus on short-term profits over long-term sustainability. The pressure to deliver quarterly results can drive companies to prioritize immediate financial gains, sometimes at the expense of ethical considerations and long-term viability. This short-termism can lead to practices such as aggressive cost-cutting, environmental degradation, and exploitative labor practices, all of which undermine the broader social and ethical responsibilities of businesses.

Another consequence is the reduction in philanthropic activities driven by religious motivations. As corporate ethics have become more secularized, the impetus for charitable giving has shifted from a sense of moral duty to strategic business considerations. While companies continue to engage in philanthropy, the motivations and underlying values have changed. This shift can lead to a more trans-actional approach to charity, where the primary goal is to enhance corporate reputation rather than to address social needs out of a genuine sense of compassion and responsibility.

Reflection Section: Ethical Dilemmas in Modern Business

Reflect on the following questions to deepen your understanding of the ethical shifts in corporate America:

- How do you perceive the balance between profit maximization and ethical responsibility in your own workplace?
- Can you identify instances where short-term financial goals have conflicted with long-term ethical considerations?
- How do you think integrating more robust ethical principles could impact the overall success and sustainability of a business?

These questions encourage you to critically evaluate the ethical dimensions of modern corporate practices, fostering a deeper under-standing of the complex interplay between profit and morality in today's business environment.

THE RISE OF CORPORATE SOCIAL RESPONSIBILITY AND ITS SECULAR FOCUS

In the early days of American enterprise, the concept of philanthropy was inseparable from the Christian ethos that permeated society. Business leaders such as John D. Rockefeller and Andrew Carnegie viewed their immense wealth as a divine trust, a means to effectuate social good in accordance with biblical imperatives. Rockefeller, for instance, believed in the principle of stewardship derived from the parable of the talents, using his fortune to establish universities, medical research institutions, and numerous charitable foundations. Carnegie, although controversially secular in some respects, still adhered to what he termed the "Gospel of Wealth," advocating for the affluent to redistribute their riches for the betterment of society. These early acts of benevolence were deeply rooted in a moral framework that identified wealth as a tool for divine service and communal upliftment.

As we moved into the 20th century, the notion of corporate social responsibility (CSR) began to formalize, influenced by the growing complexities of industrial capitalism and societal expectations. Initially, CSR initiatives retained traces of their religious origins, but over time, they evolved to reflect broader, more secular concerns. The Great Depression and subsequent New Deal policies catalyzed a shift towards more structured corporate philanthropy, emphasizing social welfare as a corporate obligation. This transition marked the beginning of CSR as an institutionalized practice, with companies adopting formal codes of ethics and establishing dedicated departments for social responsibility. The focus was no longer solely on individual acts of charity but on creating sustainable frameworks for ongoing social contributions.

In contemporary times, CSR has undergone further secularization, reflecting significant shifts in societal values. Modern CSR initiatives are primarily driven by concerns for environmental sustainability and social justice, moving away from religious motivations toward secular ethics. Environmental sustainability has become a cornerstone of CSR, with corporations committing to reducing their carbon footprints, adopting renewable energy sources, and promoting eco-friendly products. Companies like Patagonia and Tesla have built their entire business models around sustainability, viewing environmental stewardship as both a moral obligation and a competitive advantage. These initiatives are guided by a secular ethic that prioritizes the long-term health of the planet over immediate financial gains.

Social justice is another focal point of modern CSR, addressing issues such as economic inequality, labor rights, and community development. Corporations are increasingly involved in initiatives that promote social equity, from fair trade practices to philanthropic efforts aimed at alleviating poverty. The emphasis on diversity and inclusion initiatives reflects a commitment to fostering equitable workplaces and communities. This shift is evident in the proliferation of diversity training programs, equitable hiring practices, and support for marginalized groups. Companies like Ben & Jerry's and Nike have taken public stances on social justice issues, aligning their brand identities with broader societal movements for equity and inclusion.

The objectives and goals of modern CSR programs are guided by secular principles that emphasize corporate citizenship and ethical supply chains. Corporate citizenship refers to the role of businesses as responsible members of society, contributing to the common good through ethical practices and community engagement. Ethical supply chains focus on ensuring that every stage of production, from raw materials to finished products, adheres to ethical standards. This includes fair labor practices, humane treatment of workers, and environmentally sustainable operations. These principles are encapsulated in frameworks like the United Nations Global Compact, which encourages businesses to adopt sustainable and socially responsible policies.

Community engagement is another critical aspect of modern CSR, with companies striving to build positive relationships with the communities in which they operate. This involves supporting local initiatives, investing in community development projects, and fostering open dialogue with community stakeholders. Stakeholder theory, which posits that businesses should consider the interests of all stakeholders, not just shareholders, underpins this approach. By engaging with employees, customers, suppliers, and the community, companies aim to create shared value that benefits both the business and society.

The effectiveness and criticisms of secular CSR initiatives are subjects of ongoing debate. Successful CSR programs have demonstrated that ethical and sustainable practices can coexist with profitability. For example, Unilever's Sustainable Living Plan has shown that sustainable business practices can drive growth and innovation, leading to both environmental benefits and financial success. Similarly, Starbucks' commitment to ethical sourcing and community engagement has enhanced its brand reputation and customer loyalty. These case studies illustrate that CSR can be a win-win strategy, benefiting both businesses and society.

However, criticisms of CSR often focus on issues of authenticity and "greenwashing," where companies use environmental and social initiatives as a marketing tool rather than a genuine commitment to ethical practices. Skeptics argue that some corporations engage in CSR superficially, prioritizing public relations over substantive change. This criticism highlights the need for transparency and accountability in CSR initiatives, ensuring that companies' actions align with their stated commitments. The challenge for modern businesses is to integrate CSR authentically into their core operations, moving beyond token gestures to create meaningful and lasting impact.

The rise of corporate social responsibility represents a significant evolution from its religious and philanthropic roots to a secular focus on sustainability and social justice. As modern CSR initiatives continue to evolve, the challenge lies in maintaining authenticity and ensuring that ethical principles are genuinely integrated into corporate practices, benefiting both businesses and the broader society.

FAITH IN THE WORKPLACE: HISTORICAL VS. MODERN PERSPECTIVES

In the past, faith in the workplace was not merely tolerated but often encouraged. During the early days of American industry, business settings frequently accommodated and even celebrated religious expression. Employers might start the workday with a prayer or allow employees time for religious observances. This approach was rooted in the belief that a morally upright workforce, guided by Christian principles, was essential for both ethical business practices and societal well-being. Religious holidays were widely observed, and workers were often given time off to participate in religious ceremonies. The notion that faith and work were intertwined was not merely a cultural norm but a reflection of societal values emphasizing the importance of spiritual well-being and material success.

In contrast, modern corporate environments emphasize secularism and neutrality, driven by a commitment to inclusivity and the separation of personal beliefs from professional responsibilities. Today, businesses are more likely to implement policies that promote a neutral environment, free from religious influence, to ensure that employees of all faiths—or none—feel equally respected. This shift is partly a response to the increasing religious diversity within the workforce and the need to avoid potential conflicts or accusations of favoritism. Companies now focus on creating inclusive workspaces that respect individual beliefs while maintaining a professional atmosphere. This secular approach aims to foster an environment where all employees can collaborate effectively, irrespective of their religious backgrounds.

In this context, faith-based employee resource groups (ERGs) have emerged as a way to support employees' spiritual needs while maintaining workplace neutrality. These groups provide a platform for employees to share their faith, offer mutual support, and engage in religious activities within the bounds of corporate policies. For example, American Airlines, Intel, and Target have established faith-based ERGs to accommodate the spiritual needs of their employees. These groups organize activities such as prayer meetings, discussion forums, and community service projects, creating a sense of community and belonging among participants. They also serve as a resource for educating the broader workforce about religious diversity and fostering mutual respect and understanding.

The legal and regulatory landscape surrounding faith in the workplace is shaped by laws designed to protect religious freedom while ensuring workplace fairness. Title VII of the Civil Rights Act of 1964 is a cornerstone of these protections, prohibiting employment discrimination based on religion and requiring employers to provide reasonable accommodations for employees' religious practices, as long as these do not cause undue hardship for the business. The Equal Employment Opportunity Commission (EEOC) provides guidelines on religious discrimination, outlining employers' responsibilities and employees' rights. These guidelines help navigate the complex interplay between respecting religious expression and maintaining a neutral work environment, ensuring that both employers and employees understand their legal obligations and protections.

Balancing religious expression with workplace inclusivity presents both challenges and benefits. For employees, the ability to express their faith openly can enhance job satisfaction and overall well-being. It can foster a sense of community and belonging, reducing feelings of isolation and promoting mental health. However, overt religious expression can also lead to potential conflicts, especially in diverse workplaces where employees may hold differing or even conflicting beliefs. Employers must navigate these dynamics carefully, creating policies that respect individual rights while promoting a harmonious work environment. This balance requires clear communication, sensitivity to employees' needs, and a commitment to inclusivity.

Faith-based initiatives in the workplace offer significant benefits, not only for employees but also for the organization as a whole. These initiatives can improve employee morale, foster a supportive work environment, and enhance organizational loyalty. When employees feel that their spiritual needs are respected, they are more likely to be engaged and committed to their work. Moreover, faith-based ERGs can contribute to a positive corporate culture, promoting values such as integrity, compassion, and social responsibility. By supporting employees' spiritual well-being, companies can create a more holistic and inclusive workplace, benefiting both individuals and the organization.

The evolution of faith in the workplace reflects broader societal changes, from historical acceptance to modern secularism. This shift has led to the development of faith-based ERGs, the implementation of legal protections, and the pursuit of a balance between religious expression and inclusivity. As the workplace continues to evolve, the challenge lies in navigating these complexities while fostering an environment that respects and supports the diverse spiritual needs of all employees.

THE MARGINALIZATION OF RELIGIOUS EXPRESSION IN CORPORATIONS

In contemporary corporate settings, religious expression is often constrained by policies prioritizing secularism and neutrality. One prominent example is the restriction on religious attire and symbols. Many companies, striving to present a unified corporate image, impose dress codes that inadvertently or deliberately restrict employees from wearing religious garments such as hijabs, yarmulkes, or crosses. These policies are often justified under the guise of maintaining a professional appearance, yet they can marginalize those who view their religious attire as an integral part of their identity. Consider a case where a Sikh employee is denied the right to wear a turban or a Christian is asked to remove a cross necklace; such restrictions not only compromise individual expression but also signal a lack of inclusivity within the corporate environment.

Furthermore, limitations on religious discussions and activities are commonplace. Corporate policies frequently discourage or outright ban discussions on religion, citing the potential for conflict and the need to maintain a harmonious workplace. This can extend to prohibiting prayer groups or Bible study sessions during lunch breaks, relegating religious practices to the private sphere. For instance, a company might forbid employees from organizing a prayer group in a break room, arguing that such activities could alienate non-religious colleagues or those of different faiths. These limitations stifle the expression of religious identity, creating a sterile environment where employees feel compelled to compartmentalize their spirituality.

The motivations behind these policies are multifaceted, rooted in efforts to maintain a neutral and inclusive workplace. In an era characterized by increasing religious diversity, companies aim to prevent any practices that could be perceived as favoring one belief system over another. This commitment to neutrality is intended to foster an environment where all employees feel equally valued, regardless of their religious affiliations. However, this well-intentioned approach can backfire, inadvertently marginalizing those for whom religious expression is a vital aspect of daily life. Additionally, concerns about potential conflicts and discrimination play a significant role. Employers fear that visible religious practices might lead to tensions among employees or result in accusations of bias. By restricting religious expression, companies hope to preemptively address these issues, ensuring a smooth and conflict-free workplace.

The consequences of marginalizing religious expression are profound, impacting both employees and corporate culture. Employees who feel unable to express their faith at work often experience feelings of alienation and exclusion. This sense of disconnection can lead to decreased job satisfaction, lower morale, and reduced productivity. When individuals are forced to suppress an essential part of their identity, it affects their overall well-being and engagement with their work. Moreover, the potential loss of diverse perspectives and values is a significant concern. Religious beliefs often shape ethical frameworks and moral perspectives, contributing to a richer, more nuanced understanding of complex issues. By sidelining these voices, companies risk creating a homogenized culture that lacks depth and diversity of thought.

Legal and social challenges to these restrictive policies are increasingly prevalent. Numerous legal battles have been fought over religious accommodations, with employees challenging discriminatory practices through the courts. The U.S. Supreme Court's recent decision requiring employers to reasonably accommodate workers' religious practices unless it results in substantially increased costs underscores the legal impetus to protect religious expression in the workplace. Advocacy by religious freedom organizations further highlights the ongoing struggle to secure these rights. Groups such as the Becket Fund for Religious Liberty and the American Center for Law and Justice actively campaign against policies that infringe on religious freedoms, offering legal support and raising public awareness.

Efforts to protect religious expression in the workplace are crucial in navigating the delicate balance between inclusivity and individual rights. Companies must strive to create policies that respect religious diversity while maintaining a cohesive and professional environment. This involves not only adhering to legal requirements but also fostering a corporate culture that genuinely values and accommodates diverse beliefs. Such an approach can enhance employee well-being, foster a more inclusive workplace, and ultimately contribute to a more dynamic and innovative corporate culture.

CASE STUDIES: CORPORATIONS THAT HAVE EMBRACED OR REJECTED CHRISTIAN VALUES

Consider the case of Chick-fil-A, a company whose corporate culture is deeply rooted in Christian values, influencing its business practices and community involvement. Founded by S. Truett Cathy in 1967, Chick-fil-A has consistently integrated faith into its operations. The company is famously closed on Sundays to allow employees a day of rest and worship, a policy that reflects Cathy's commitment to observing the Sabbath. Furthermore, Chick-fil-A's corporate headquarters are adorned with Christian symbols and artwork, and the company's cups often feature Bible quotes. This religious ethos extends to their philanthropic efforts, which include funding scholarships and community projects that align with their values. However, the company has faced significant challenges and criticisms, particularly regarding its stance on LGBTQ+ issues. Public backlash and boycotts have arisen in response to donations made to organizations perceived as anti-LGBTQ+, leading to a complex interplay between maintaining religious principles and navigating public opinion.

Hobby Lobby, another corporation that openly embraces Christian values, provides a compelling example of faith-based business practices. Founded by David Green in 1972, Hobby Lobby operates on principles derived from biblical teachings. The company's stores are closed on Sundays, and employees receive above-average wages, reflecting the belief in fair treatment and respect for workers. Hobby Lobby's commitment to faith is also evident in its legal battles, most notably the Supreme Court case Burwell v. Hobby Lobby Stores, Inc. The company successfully argued for an exemption from a federal mandate requiring employer-provided health insurance to cover contraceptives, citing religious objections. While this victory affirmed their religious rights, it also sparked widespread debate and criticism, highlighting the tensions between religious freedom and public health mandates.

Interstate Batteries offers yet another illustration of integrating faith and business. Founded by John Searcy and headquartered in Dallas,

Texas, the company has woven Christian values into its corporate fabric. Interstate Batteries holds weekly chapels for employees, encourages prayer at the beginning of meetings, and supports numerous faith-based initiatives. Their mission statement explicitly references their commitment to "honoring God" while serving customers and stakeholders. Despite these practices, the company navigates the challenges of maintaining a balance between religious expression and inclusivity, striving to respect diverse beliefs within its workforce.

However, not all corporations have maintained a religious foundation. Apple Inc., for instance, has firmly embraced secular CSR initiatives, focusing on environmental sustainability, ethical supply chains, and human rights. Under the leadership of Tim Cook, Apple has prioritized reducing its carbon footprint, achieving significant milestones in renewable energy use and waste reduction. The company's charitable giving is oriented towards global health, education, and disaster relief, reflecting a commitment to secular humanitarian principles. Apple's approach underscores a shift towards a more inclusive and global perspective, distancing itself from any specific religious affiliation.

Google, similarly, places a strong emphasis on diversity and inclusion, fostering an environment where all employees feel welcome, regardless of their religious beliefs. The company's initiatives include comprehensive diversity training, support for various employee resource groups, and policies that promote an inclusive workplace culture. Google's focus on creating a neutral and secular environment is evident in its approach to community engagement and corporate responsibility. While these practices have garnered praise for promoting equality and inclusivity, they also illustrate a departure from any religious framework, reflecting a broader societal trend towards secularism.

The decisions to embrace or reject Christian values have profound implications for corporate reputation and success. Chick-fil-A's steadfast adherence to its religious principles has fostered a loyal customer base, but it has also led to public controversies and boycotts. Similarly, Hobby Lobby's commitment to faith-based practices has strengthened its identity but has also sparked legal and social challenges. Conversely, companies like Apple and Google, which have moved away from religious affiliations, have cultivated a reputation for inclusivity and progressive values. These decisions have enhanced their brand perception and financial performance, positioning them as leaders in corporate responsibility.

In examining these case studies, it becomes evident that the integration or rejection of Christian values significantly impacts corporate culture, public perception, and market success. As we transition to the next chapter, we will explore the broader societal implications of these shifts, considering how the evolving relationship between faith and commerce shapes our understanding of ethics, responsibility, and community in the modern world.

THE CONSEQUENCES OF SECULARIZATION

When walking through the bustling streets of modern cities, one cannot help but notice a transformation that has quietly crept into the fabric of our society. Billboards advertise material success, while public discourse increasingly gravitates towards secular ideologies. This shift is not merely cosmetic but indicative of a deeper, more profound change: the erosion of moral and ethical standards that were once steadfastly underpinned by Christian principles.

THE EROSION OF MORAL AND ETHICAL STANDARDS

In analyzing the decline of moral and ethical standards in secular societies, it becomes evident that as we move away from Christian principles, societal norms have undergone significant transformations. The increasing acceptance of behaviors previously considered immoral is a testament to this shift. Actions such as dishonesty, promiscuity, and even forms of exploitation have found greater acceptance or, at the very least, a reduction in societal censure. The normalization of such behaviors can be traced to a broader cultural embrace of moral relativism, where the absolutes once provided by Christian ethics are replaced by subjective interpretations of right and wrong.

Legal standards, too, have reflected this shift towards secular values. Historical legal systems, heavily influenced by Judeo-Christian ethics, emphasized justice, fairness, and the intrinsic worth of the individual. However, contemporary legal frameworks often prioritize individual freedoms and rights, sometimes at the expense of collective moral accountability. This change is evident in landmark legal decisions that have redefined traditional understandings of marriage, family, and personal autonomy. While these changes promote inclusivity and personal liberty, they also contribute to a landscape where ethical boundaries become increasingly fluid.

Christian ethics have historically played a crucial role in maintaining societal moral standards. Biblical principles have served as a moral compass, guiding both personal and societal behavior. The Ten Commandments, with their clear directives against theft, murder, and deceit, provided a foundational ethical framework for centuries. The teachings of Jesus, particularly the Sermon on the Mount, emphasized virtues such as humility, mercy, and peacemaking, fostering a culture of compassion and integrity. Christian leaders, from Augustine to Aquinas, have engaged in moral debates, shaping the ethical discourse of their times and beyond. Their influence extended into the realms of law, politics, and education, ensuring that moral considerations remained at the forefront of societal development.

The erosion of these ethical standards can be seen in the rise of corporate scandals and unethical business practices. High-profile cases, such as the Enron collapse and the 2008 financial crisis, are stark reminders of what happens when greed and deceit override moral integrity. These scandals not only caused significant economic damage but also eroded public trust in institutions that were once considered pillars of society. The prevalence of white-collar crimes, including fraud and embezzlement, further under-scores this ethical decline. Data from the Association of Certified Fraud Examiners reveals that occupational fraud alone results in billions of dollars in losses annually, reflecting a pervasive culture of dishonesty in the corporate world.

Moreover, the increase in crimes such as fraud and corruption is symptomatic of a broader societal malaise. When ethical standards are diluted, individuals are more likely to engage in behavior priori-tizing personal gain over communal well-being. This shift has a cascading effect, influencing everything from everyday interper-sonal interactions to the functioning of major institutions. The erosion of moral standards leads to decreased trust among individ-uals and institutions. When people perceive that ethical behavior is no longer valued or rewarded, cynicism and skepticism take root. This decline in trust has profound implications for social cohesion, as trust is a fundamental component of healthy relationships and communities.

Interpersonal relationships suffer as ethical erosion takes its toll. In a society where moral relativism prevails, commitments and promises lose their sanctity. Marriages, friendships, and profes-sional relationships are increasingly seen as transactional, driven by convenience rather than genuine commitment. This shift impacts the very fabric of community dynamics, weakening the bonds that hold society together. Community dynamics also change as ethical erosion fosters a culture of individualism. The collective responsibility that once characterized communal life gives way to a more atomized existence, where personal success is often prioritized over collective well-being. This cultural shift undermines the sense of belonging and mutual support essential for vibrant communities.

As we navigate these complexities, it is essential to recognize that the erosion of moral and ethical standards is not merely an abstract phenomenon but a tangible reality with far-reaching consequences. The decline in societal trust, changes in interpersonal relationships, and the weakening of community dynamics all point to the need for a reassessment of the values that underpin our collective lives. This chapter has explored the multifaceted impact of secularization on moral and ethical standards, highlighting the challenges and opportunities that lie ahead.

THE RISE OF SECULAR HUMANISM

As you stroll through the corridors of intellectual history, you will find that the rise of secular humanism is a narrative rich with pivotal moments and philosophical evolution. Rooted in the Enlightenment, this paradigm emerged as a direct challenge to the religious orthodoxy that had long dominated European thought. Enlightenment thinkers such as Voltaire, Diderot, and Rousseau championed reason and empirical inquiry, rejecting the idea that religious authority should dictate moral and intellectual life. This intellectual rebellion laid the groundwork for secular humanism, emphasizing the capacity of human reason to discern truth and morality independently of divine revelation.

The formation of humanist organizations and the drafting of manifestos in the 20th century further solidified secular humanism as a coherent worldview. The Humanist Manifesto I, published in 1933, marked a significant milestone, articulating a vision of a progressive society grounded in human welfare and rational ethics. This document, followed by subsequent manifestos, outlined a philosophy that sought to address human needs and aspirations without recourse to supernatural explanations. Humanist organizations like the American Humanist Association played a crucial role in promoting these ideals, advocating for a society where ethical living is informed by reason, compassion, and a commitment to human rights.

At its core, secular humanism is anchored in a set of philosophical principles that prioritize reason, science, and human rights. It rejects supernatural beliefs and religious dogma, positing that human beings can achieve moral and intellectual fulfillment through rational inquiry and empirical evidence. This stance is not merely a negation of religious belief but a positive affirmation of human potential and dignity. Secular humanists argue that ethical principles should be derived from human experience and scientific understanding rather than divine commandments. This emphasis on reason and science fosters a dynamic and adaptable worldview capable of responding to new discoveries and changing social conditions.

The influence of secular humanism on contemporary society is profound and multifaceted. In education, it has led to curricula that emphasize critical thinking, scientific literacy, and ethical reasoning. Schools and universities increasingly adopt secular humanist principles, fostering environments where students are encouraged to question assumptions and explore diverse perspectives. This shift has not only enriched academic inquiry but also promoted a more inclusive and pluralistic educational landscape.

Scientific research, too, has been profoundly shaped by secular humanism. The rejection of supernatural explanations has paved the way for methodological naturalism, the cornerstone of modern scientific inquiry. This approach, which relies on observable and testable phenomena, has driven advancements in fields ranging from biology to cosmology. The secular humanist commitment to empirical evidence and rational analysis has thus been instrumental in expanding our understanding of the natural world.

Cultural and social movements have also felt the impact of secular humanism. The emphasis on human rights and social justice has inspired activism aimed at addressing inequality, discrimination, and other societal ills. Movements advocating for gender equality, LGBTQ+ rights, and secular governance draw heavily on humanist principles, seeking to create a more just and equitable society. This influence extends to the arts and humanities, where secular humanist themes often explore the complexities of the human condition and the pursuit of meaning in a world without divine oversight.

Despite its contributions, secular humanism faces significant criticisms and challenges. Religious communities often contend that secular humanism lacks a transcendent moral foundation, leading to ethical relativism and a diminished sense of meaning. Critics argue that without belief in a higher power, moral and ethical standards become arbitrary, undermining social cohesion and stability. These concerns reflect broader debates about the role of religion in public life and the sources of moral authority.

Internal debates persist within the humanist movement itself. Some humanists advocate for a more inclusive approach that recognizes the value of religious traditions in fostering community and ethical behavior. Others maintain a staunchly secular stance, emphasizing the need to separate religious beliefs from public policy and education. These internal tensions highlight the dynamic and evolving nature of secular humanism as it seeks to balance its commitment to reason and science with the complexities of human experience and societal needs.

As you reflect on these developments, consider the ways in which secular humanism has reshaped our intellectual and cultural landscape, challenging us to rethink the foundations of ethics and the sources of meaning in our lives.

MENTAL HEALTH AND SPIRITUAL WELL-BEING: A CORRELATION?

The intricate relationship between mental health and spiritual well-being has long been a subject of scholarly inquiry, revealing compelling evidence that religious practices can significantly enhance psychological resilience. Various studies demonstrate that individuals who engage in regular religious practices, such as prayer, meditation, and communal worship, tend to exhibit lower levels of anxiety and depression. These practices offer a structured framework for individuals to process their emotions, providing a sense of purpose and belonging that is often absent in secular contexts. The act of engaging in communal rituals, for instance, fosters social connections and support networks, which are crucial for mental well-being. Moreover, the teachings and narratives found in religious texts offer coping mechanisms for life's adversities, encouraging a perspective that transcends immediate suffering.

As secularization advances, the mental health landscape undergoes marked changes, presenting unique challenges. The decline in religious participation correlates with an increase in feelings of isolation and existential anxiety. Without the communal and existential support traditionally provided by religious institutions, individuals may struggle to find meaning and purpose. This existential vacuum can contribute to higher rates of mental health disorders, such as depression and anxiety, as individuals grapple with the pressures of modern life without the scaffolding of faith. The secular emphasis on individualism and material success further exacerbates these challenges, often leading to a sense of disconnection and alienation. In a society where material achievements frequently measure success, the absence of a spiritual framework can leave individuals feeling unmoored and unsupported.

Religious communities have historically played a pivotal role in offering mental health support, providing services that extend beyond the purely spiritual. Church-based counseling services, for example, offer a unique blend of psychological and spiritual guidance, addressing both the emotional and existential dimensions of mental health. These services often incorporate elements of pastoral care, where trained clergy provide counseling that integrates theological insights with psychological principles. Support groups within religious congregations also offer a safe and empathetic space for individuals to share their struggles, fostering a sense of community and mutual support. Community outreach programs, such as those run by religious charities, provide essential services, including crisis intervention, addiction recovery programs, and support for the bereaved, addressing the multifaceted needs of individuals in distress.

In secular societies, alternative approaches to mental health have emerged to fill the void left by the decline of religious institutions. Secular therapy and counseling services, grounded in evidence-based practices, offer professional support for mental health issues. These services often employ cognitive-behavioral techniques, mindfulness practices, and other therapeutic modalities to address psychological distress. Community mental health programs, funded by government and non-profit organizations, provide accessible and affordable mental health care to diverse populations. These programs aim to promote mental well-being through preventative measures, early intervention, and comprehensive treatment plans. Secular initiatives also emphasize the importance of social support networks, recognizing that community engagement and social connections are crucial for mental health.

The correlation between mental health and spiritual well-being is complex and multifaceted, reflecting the profound impact of secularization on psychological resilience and community support. While religious practices offer a structured framework for coping with life's challenges, the decline in religious participation presents unique mental health challenges. Religious communities continue to play a vital role in providing mental health support, while secular approaches offer alternative pathways to well-being. This interplay between religious and secular approaches highlights the need for a nuanced understanding of mental health, recognizing the diverse factors that contribute to psychological resilience and community cohesion. As we navigate these complexities, it is essential to consider the ways in which spiritual and secular frameworks can coexist, offering complementary support for individuals in their pursuit of mental well-being.

COMMUNITY AND SOCIAL COHESION IN A SECULAR SOCIETY

As the influence of religion wanes, the dynamics within communities undergo significant transformations, particularly in terms of social cohesion. The reduction in community-based activities and gatherings is a stark indicator of this shift. Historically, religious institutions served as the epicenters of social life, organizing events that brought people together. From weekly services to seasonal festivals, these gatherings fostered a sense of belonging and community spirit. In the absence of these regular, faith-based activities, secular societies often struggle to replicate the same level of communal engagement and unity. The decline in volunteerism and charitable giving further exacerbates this issue. Religious teachings often emphasize the importance of altruism and service to others, compelling congregants to volunteer their time and resources. With the decline of religious influence, these motivations wane, leading to a tangible decrease in community participation and support for charitable causes.

Religious institutions have historically played a pivotal role in fostering social cohesion. Churches, synagogues, mosques, and temples have long served as community centers, providing not only spiritual guidance but also social support networks. These institutions often organize social events, educational programs, and support groups, creating spaces where individuals can connect and build relationships. Religious festivals and events, such as Christmas, Easter, Ramadan, and Diwali, have traditionally promoted social bonds, offering opportunities for communal celebration and collective identity. These gatherings are more than mere rituals; they are vital mechanisms for reinforcing social ties and fostering a sense of shared purpose and belonging.

Building a community in secular societies presents unique challenges, often marked by a decline in social trust and an increase in individualism. Without the unifying framework of shared religious beliefs and practices, secular communities must find alternative ways to foster cohesion. The rise of individualism, driven by a cultural emphasis on personal autonomy and success, often undermines efforts to create inclusive and cohesive communities. Data from sociological studies indicate a troubling trend: as religious participation declines, social trust diminishes, making it harder to build and sustain strong, interconnected communities. The challenge lies in creating spaces where diverse individuals can come together, form meaningful connections, and work towards common goals, despite the absence of a unifying religious framework.

However, successful secular initiatives demonstrate that it is possible to promote social cohesion without relying on religious institutions. Secular community centers and events play a crucial role in this regard, offering spaces for people to gather, share experiences, and support one another. These centers often host a variety of activities, from cultural events and educational workshops to recreational programs and social services. Government initiatives also contribute to social integration, implementing policies and programs designed to foster community engagement and inclusivity. Examples include public funding for community centers, support for volunteer organizations, and initiatives to promote civic participation and social responsibility.

Successful secular initiatives highlight the potential for creating cohesive communities in the absence of religious institutions. Programs that focus on shared values, such as empathy, respect, and mutual support, can bridge the gap left by the decline of religion. Community centers, for instance, often serve as hubs for social interaction, offering a range of activities and services that cater to diverse interests and needs. Events such as neighborhood fairs, cultural festivals, and public lectures provide opportunities for individuals to come together, celebrate their differences, and build a sense of collective identity. Government policies that promote social integration, such as funding for community projects and support for volunteer organizations, further enhance these efforts, creating an environment where social cohesion can thrive.

In examining the changes in community dynamics with the decline of religion, it becomes clear that the impact on social cohesion is profound and multifaceted. The reduction in community-based activities and gatherings, coupled with changes in volunteerism and charitable giving, underscores the challenges faced by secular societies. However, the role of religious institutions in fostering social cohesion highlights the potential for alternative approaches. By learning from successful secular initiatives and implementing policies that promote social integration, it is possible to create inclusive and cohesive communities that thrive in a secular context.

THE ROLE OF RELIGION IN ADDRESSING SOCIAL ISSUES

Throughout history, religion has been a formidable force in social reform movements, often serving as the moral bedrock upon which calls for justice and equality have been built. The abolitionist movement in the 19th century stands as a profound testament to the influence of Christian leaders in the fight against slavery. Figures such as William Wilberforce and Harriet Beecher Stowe mobilized biblical teachings to challenge the moral legitimacy of human bondage. Wilberforce's relentless advocacy in the British Parliament was deeply rooted in his Christian convictions, while Stowe's novel, "Uncle Tom's Cabin," invoked Christian imagery to galvanize public sentiment against the inhumanity of slavery. These leaders did not merely draw from faith as a source of personal strength but wielded it as a powerful tool for societal transformation.

The Civil Rights Movement of the mid-20th century further exemplifies the pivotal role of religious organizations in advocating for social change. Dr. Martin Luther King Jr., a Baptist minister, articulated his vision of racial equality through the lens of Christian theology. His "Letter from Birmingham Jail" eloquently argued that injustice anywhere is a threat to justice everywhere, using biblical references to underscore the moral imperative for civil disobedience against unjust laws. Churches served as sanctuaries for organizing protests, offering spiritual and logistical support to activists. The Southern Christian Leadership Conference (SCLC) and other faith-based organizations were instrumental in mobilizing communities and fostering a collective resolve to dismantle segregation and achieve civil rights for African Americans.

In contemporary times, religious initiatives continue to address pressing social issues with remarkable efficacy. Faith-based organizations are at the forefront of poverty alleviation efforts, providing essential services such as food, shelter, and healthcare to marginalized populations. Organizations like Catholic Charities and the Salvation Army engage in multifaceted programs that address both immediate needs and long-term solutions, emphasizing the dignity and worth of every individual. These initiatives are often driven by a theological commitment to social justice, reflecting the biblical call to care for the "least of these."

Religious groups also play a significant role in advocating for social justice and human rights. Faith-based advocacy organizations, such as Sojourners and the Interfaith Center on Corporate Responsibility, work to influence public policy on issues ranging from economic inequality to environmental stewardship. These groups draw on their moral and ethical frameworks to challenge systemic injustices, advocating for policies that promote equity and sustainability. Their efforts extend beyond charity, aiming to transform the structures that perpetuate poverty and oppression.

When comparing the effectiveness of religious versus secular approaches to social issues, it is essential to consider the unique contributions of each. Data and case studies reveal that faith-based programs often achieve significant outcomes due to their holistic approach and deep community ties. For instance, a study by the University of Pennsylvania found that faith-based organizations are highly effective in reducing recidivism rates among formerly incarcerated individuals, owing to their emphasis on spiritual rehabilitation and community support. Similarly, religious motivation often enhances volunteerism and activism, as individuals are inspired by their faith to engage in selfless service and advocacy.

Secular programs, on the other hand, bring valuable expertise in areas such as policy analysis, scientific research, and professional service delivery. These initiatives benefit from a focus on evidence-based practices and a commitment to inclusivity, ensuring that services are accessible to all, regardless of religious affiliation. However, the absence of a unifying moral framework can sometimes limit the depth of community engagement and the sense of shared purpose that are hallmarks of faith-based efforts.

The potential for collaboration between religious and secular groups offers a promising avenue for addressing social issues more comprehensively. Interfaith and inter-organizational partnerships can leverage the strengths of both approaches, fostering innovative solutions and broad-based support. Collaborative initiatives, such as the interfaith Climate Action Network, demonstrate how diverse groups can unite around common goals, pooling resources and expertise to tackle complex challenges. These partnerships not only enhance the effectiveness of social programs but also promote mutual understanding and respect among different communities.

As we consider the role of religion in addressing social issues, it is clear that faith-based efforts have made, and continue to make, significant contributions to societal well-being. The historical and contemporary examples of religious engagement in social reform highlight the enduring relevance of faith in public life. By fostering collaboration between religious and secular groups, we can build on these foundations to create a more just and compassionate society. This exploration of the interplay between faith and social issues sets the stage for a deeper examination of how these dynamics influence other aspects of contemporary life.

INTERFAITH DIALOGUE AND ITS ROLE IN MODERN AMERICA

Imagine a bustling city square where people of diverse faiths gather not to protest but to engage in meaningful dialogue. This is not a utopian dream but a reality in several parts of the world, where interfaith dialogue serves as a powerful tool for fostering social harmony and mutual respect in an increasingly pluralistic society. In an era marked by global interconnectedness, the necessity of interfaith dialogue cannot be overstated. It transcends mere tolerance, promoting a deeper understanding and appreciation of different religious traditions.

Interfaith dialogue is pivotal for reducing religious tensions and conflicts. When individuals from diverse faith backgrounds come together to discuss their beliefs and practices, they demystify the 'other,' breaking down stereotypes and prejudices. This mutual understanding fosters an environment where differences are not merely tolerated but respected. For instance, Hartford International University for Religion and Peace emphasizes that explaining one's faith to others not only deepens one's own understanding but also fosters empathy and respect. This continuous dialogue is essential for resolving conflicts and promoting peace, as learning about other religions expands knowledge and understanding, thereby reducing religious tensions and conflicts.

Moreover, interfaith dialogue plays a crucial role in preventing religious extremism. By creating platforms for open and honest conversations, it addresses the root causes of radicalization. Youth, often susceptible to extremist ideologies, can be guided towards a more inclusive understanding of faith through dialogue initiatives. For example, programs aimed at preventing youth radicalization usually involve interfaith workshops and discussions, where young individuals from different religious backgrounds share their experiences and learn from each other. Such initiatives provide them with a broader perspective, countering the narrow, exclusionary narratives propagated by extremist groups. Case studies of successful deradicalization programs further underscore the effectiveness of interfaith dialogue. In these programs, former extremists often cite the transformative power of engaging with individuals from diverse faith backgrounds as a key factor in their journey towards renouncing violence and embracing peace.

The benefits of interfaith dialogue extend beyond preventing extremism; they significantly enhance community development. Collaborative community service projects, for instance, bring together individuals from different faiths to work towards a common goal, fostering a sense of unity and shared purpose. These projects not only address immediate community needs but also build lasting relationships among participants, creating a strong, cohesive community. Interfaith forums and discussion groups further contribute to community cohesion by providing safe spaces for individuals to express their beliefs, discuss common challenges, and explore shared values. These forums often culminate in joint initiatives that reflect the collective aspirations of the community, reinforcing the bonds formed through dialogue.

However, promoting effective interfaith dialogue is not without its challenges. Deep-seated prejudices and stereotypes often pose significant barriers. Many individuals grow up with preconceived notions about other religions, shaped by cultural and societal influences. Overcoming these biases requires a concerted effort to foster open-mindedness and empathy. Interfaith dialogue must be approached with humility, and a willingness to listen, as genuine understanding, can only be achieved through respectful and empathetic engagement. Navigating theological differences also presents a challenge. While finding common ground is essential, it is equally important to acknowledge and respect the distinct beliefs and practices of each faith. This delicate balance requires skillful facilitation and a commitment to maintaining an open, non-judgmental atmosphere.

Despite these challenges, the potential for interfaith dialogue to transform communities and promote social harmony is immense. By reducing religious tensions, preventing extremism, and enhancing community cohesion, interfaith dialogue lays the foundation for a more inclusive and peaceful society. The journey towards achieving this vision is fraught with challenges, but the rewards are well worth the effort. Engaging in interfaith dialogue not only enriches our understanding of others but also deepens our own faith, fostering a sense of shared humanity that transcends religious boundaries. As we navigate the complexities of a diverse and interconnected world, the importance of interfaith dialogue cannot be overstated. It is a powerful tool for bridging divides, fostering mutual respect, and building a more harmonious society.

Reflection Section

Consider the following questions to reflect on your views about interfaith dialogue:

1. How have your interactions with individuals of different faiths shaped your understanding of your own beliefs?
2. What are some common stereotypes or prejudices you have encountered about your faith, and how have you addressed them?
3. Imagine participating in an interfaith dialogue. What aspects of your faith would you share, and what would you hope to learn from others?
4. How can you contribute to promoting interfaith dialogue in your community? Are there existing initiatives you can join or new ones you can start?

COMMON GROUNDS: CHRISTIANITY AND OTHER MAJOR RELIGIONS

In the vast tapestry of the world's faith traditions, certain ethical and moral principles stand as common threads, weaving a fabric of shared values that transcend doctrinal boundaries. Among these, the Golden Rule emerges as a universal axiom, resonating across Christianity, Islam, and Buddhism. In Christianity, the directive "Do unto others as you would have them do unto you" (Matthew 7:12) encapsulates the essence of ethical reciprocity. Islam echoes this sentiment in the Hadith of Prophet Muhammad: "None of you truly believes until he loves for his brother what he loves for himself." Buddhism, though differing fundamentally in its meta-physical outlook, similarly advocates for compassion and empathy through the principle of metta, or loving-kindness, urging adherents to treat all beings with the same benevolence they desire for themselves. This convergence of ethical teachings underscores a profound commonality, suggesting that, despite theological divergences, these religions embrace a shared commitment to fostering compassion, empathy, and mutual respect.

Spiritual practices across various religions further illustrate these shared values, highlighting rituals that, while distinct in form, serve similar spiritual functions. Fasting, for instance, is a practice observed in Christianity, Islam, and Hinduism, each tradition attributing unique significance to the act. Christians observe Lent, a period of fasting and penance leading up to Easter, as a time for reflection and spiritual renewal. In Islam, the holy month of Ramadan involves a month-long fast from dawn to dusk, emphasizing self-discipline, empathy for the less fortunate, and spiritual purification. Hinduism, with its diverse practices, includes fasting during various religious festivals and personal vows, serving as a means of attaining spiritual merit and deepening one's devotion. These practices, though varied in their specific observances, share a common purpose of fostering spiritual growth, self-discipline, and a heightened awareness of the divine.

Prayer and meditation also serve as universal spiritual practices, albeit with variations that reflect the distinct theological frameworks of each religion. Christianity emphasizes prayer as a means of communicating with God, seeking guidance, expressing gratitude, and interceding for others. Islam prescribes Salat, the ritual prayers performed five times a day, as a fundamental pillar of faith, fostering a continuous connection with Allah and reinforcing the believer's submission to divine will. Buddhism, while eschewing the concept of a personal deity, incorporates meditation as a central practice aimed at cultivating mindfulness, inner peace, and insight into the nature of existence. These practices, whether directed towards a personal deity or towards achieving inner enlightenment, underscore a shared pursuit of spiritual fulfillment and transcendence.

Theological similarities and differences among these religions offer a rich field for comparative analysis. Christianity, Islam, and Judaism, as monotheistic faiths, share the belief in a single, omnipotent God, yet their conceptions of the divine and their theological narratives diverge significantly. Christianity's doctrine of the Trinity posits a triune God—Father, Son, and Holy Spirit—unique among monotheistic traditions. Islam vehemently rejects this notion, upholding the absolute oneness of God (Tawhid) and viewing any division of the divine nature as blasphemous. Judaism, while sharing the monotheistic foundation, diverges from both Christianity and Islam in its theological and ritualistic traditions.

Concepts of the afterlife also illustrate both commonalities and divergences. Christianity posits a dichotomous afterlife, with eternal salvation in heaven or damnation in hell based on one's faith in Jesus Christ and adherence to God's commandments. Islam similarly envisions a final judgment, where individuals are rewarded with paradise or condemned to hell based on their deeds and faith in Allah. Buddhism, contrastingly, subscribes to the doctrine of rebirth and karma, rejecting the notion of eternal damnation or salvation, instead emphasizing the cyclical nature of existence and the pursuit of enlightenment to escape the cycle of suffering.

Historical interactions between these religions have ranged from syncretism to conflict, reflecting the complex dynamics of religious coexistence. Syncretism, the blending of religious practices and beliefs, is evident in various historical contexts. For instance, the spread of Islam in regions with pre-existing Christian and indigenous religious traditions often led to a synthesis of practices, as seen in the development of Sufi traditions that integrated elements of local spirituality. Similarly, the early spread of Christianity encountered and assimilated aspects of Greco-Roman religious practices, contributing to the rich tapestry of Christian liturgy and iconography.

However, history also records periods of religious conflict and collaboration. The Crusades, a series of religious wars between Christians and Muslims, epitomize the violent clashes stemming from theological and territorial disputes. Conversely, the intellectual exchanges during the Islamic Golden Age, where Muslim scholars engaged with Christian and Jewish intellectuals, highlight moments of profound collaboration and mutual enrichment. Such interactions, whether marked by conflict or cooperation, have indelibly shaped the development and evolution of these faith traditions, underscoring the intricate interplay of religious identities throughout history.

INTERFAITH INITIATIVES IN SCHOOLS AND COMMUNITIES

In the vibrant halls of educational institutions, interfaith initiatives have become pivotal in fostering religious understanding and respect among students. One such successful example is the establishment of interfaith clubs and student organizations. These clubs, often formed with the support of school administrations, provide a safe space for students of diverse religious backgrounds to engage in meaningful dialogue. They organize events such as interfaith dinners, panel discussions, and cultural exchange programs, where students share their beliefs and traditions. These interactions not only promote mutual respect but also encourage students to view religious diversity as an asset rather than a barrier.

Curricula that include comparative religion studies further bolster these efforts. By incorporating courses that explore the tenets, histories, and cultural contexts of various religions, schools can provide students with a well-rounded education that acknowledges the complexity of global faith traditions. These courses often involve critical analysis and discussions, encouraging students to reflect on their own beliefs while understanding others'. For instance, a world religions class might cover the core beliefs of Hinduism, Buddhism, Christianity, Islam, and Judaism, allowing students to draw parallels and appreciate the unique aspects of each faith. Such academic exposure fosters an environment where religious literacy becomes an integral part of students' intellectual and moral development.

Educators play a crucial role in fostering interfaith dialogue within the classroom. Professional development programs for teachers on interfaith education equip them with the necessary tools and knowledge to facilitate these discussions effectively. These programs often include workshops on cultural competency, religious literacy, and conflict resolution, enabling teachers to create inclusive learning environments. Classroom activities designed to promote religious literacy, such as role-playing exercises, debate sessions, and collaborative projects, further enhance these efforts. By creating opportunities for students to engage with diverse perspectives, educators help dismantle prejudices and build a foundation of mutual respect and understanding.

Community-based interfaith initiatives extend these efforts beyond the confines of educational institutions, bringing together diverse religious groups to work towards common goals. Interfaith councils and community forums are exemplary programs that provide platforms for dialogue and collaboration. These councils often comprise representatives from various religious communities who meet regularly to discuss issues affecting their neighborhoods and to devise collective solutions. Community forums, on the other hand, offer a more public space for individuals to share their experiences and engage in open discussions about faith and coexistence. These initiatives foster a sense of unity and shared purpose, emphasizing the common values that bind different faith traditions.

Collaborative social service projects are another effective means of promoting interfaith cooperation. Projects such as food drives, environmental clean-ups, and disaster relief efforts bring together individuals from different religious backgrounds to address pressing social issues. By working side by side, participants not only contribute to the betterment of their communities but also build lasting relationships based on trust and mutual respect. These collaborations highlight the practical benefits of interfaith dialogue, demonstrating that diverse religious groups can come together to achieve common objectives.

The outcomes of interfaith initiatives for participants are profound, as evidenced by numerous studies and case examples. Increased tolerance and reduced prejudices are among the most significant benefits. Participants often report a greater appreciation for religious diversity and a willingness to engage with individuals from different faith backgrounds. Data from various programs indicate that interfaith dialogue leads to enhanced empathy and understanding, breaking down stereotypes and fostering a more inclusive society. For instance, a study on interfaith programs in educational institutions found that students involved in these initiatives displayed higher levels of social cohesion and lower levels of religious prejudice compared to their peers.

Enhanced community cooperation and social cohesion are additional positive outcomes. Interfaith initiatives create networks of support and collaboration that strengthen the social fabric of communities. Participants often become advocates for interfaith dialogue, promoting its importance within their social circles and encouraging others to engage in similar initiatives. These efforts contribute to a more harmonious and resilient society where individuals are united by their shared commitment to understanding and respecting one another's beliefs.

The transformative power of interfaith dialogue in schools and communities is evident in the numerous successful initiatives that have fostered religious understanding and cooperation. By providing platforms for dialogue, education, and collaboration, these programs dismantle prejudices, build mutual respect, and create cohesive communities. The role of educators, the integration of comparative religion studies, and the impact of community-based initiatives underscore the multi-faceted approach required to promote interfaith understanding in a diverse society.

ADDRESSING MISCONCEPTIONS AND BIASES AGAINST CHRISTIANITY

The landscape of modern discourse is rife with misconceptions and stereotypes about Christianity, often rooted in misunderstandings of its doctrines and practices. Many people erroneously perceive Christianity as monolithic, failing to appreciate the rich diversity of beliefs and practices within the faith. For instance, the doctrine of the Trinity is frequently misunderstood, leading to the erroneous belief that Christians worship three gods rather than one. Similarly, the concept of salvation through grace is often misconstrued as a license for moral laxity, ignoring the rigorous ethical demands that accompany this belief. Historical events, such as the Crusades and the Inquisition, have further shaped negative perceptions, casting Christianity as inherently intolerant and violent. These events, while complex and multifaceted, are frequently oversimplified, reinforcing harmful stereotypes.

Media representation plays a significant role in shaping public perceptions of Christianity. Portrayals in movies and television often perpetuate stereotypes, such as the "Christian extremist" who holds radical viewpoints and engages in extreme actions. Characters like the prison warden in "The Shawshank Redemption," who mistreats prisoners while distributing Bibles, exemplify this trope. Similarly, the "fallen Christian," depicted as someone who loses traditional Christian morals through temptation or sin, is a recurring theme in popular culture. Quinn Fabray from "Glee," a devout Christian who faces consequences after becoming pregnant, illustrates this stereotype. Media coverage of religious events and controversies often frames these issues in terms of culture wars and politics, emphasizing conflict and drama at the expense of nuanced understanding. This tendency to present Christians as intolerant, racist, or violent is not based on truth but serves to generate profit by appealing to mass media values of conflict and drama.

Addressing and correcting these misconceptions requires a multifaceted approach. Educational campaigns and public awareness programs can play a crucial role in countering biases. These initiatives should aim to provide accurate information about Christian doctrines and practices, highlighting the diversity within the faith and dispelling common myths. Interfaith dialogues and discussions are also invaluable in clarifying misunderstandings. By engaging with individuals from different religious backgrounds, Christians can provide firsthand insights into their beliefs and practices, fostering mutual understanding and respect. These dialogues should be approached with humility and openness, emphasizing shared values and common goals while acknowledging theological differences.

Christian organizations have a pivotal role to play in promoting positive engagement and addressing misconceptions. Outreach programs and community service projects are effective means of demonstrating the practical implications of Christian ethics. By actively engaging in initiatives that address social issues, such as poverty alleviation, environmental conservation, and disaster relief, Christians can showcase the compassionate and altruistic aspects of their faith. These efforts not only benefit the broader community but also challenge negative stereotypes by presenting a more accurate and positive image of Christianity. Interfaith dialogues organized by Christian groups further contribute to this goal. By creating platforms for open and respectful conversations, these initiatives foster a deeper understanding of Christian beliefs and practices while promoting mutual respect and cooperation.

Christian organizations like the Hartford International University for Religion and Peace exemplify these efforts. Hosting conferences that bring together religious leaders from diverse backgrounds, such as Muslim and Jewish chaplains, they create opportunities for meaningful dialogue and collaboration. Programs like the Master of Arts in Interreligious Studies offered by the university further reinforce these efforts by providing academic and practical training in interfaith engagement. Through these initiatives, Christian organizations can play a crucial role in addressing misconceptions and promoting a more nuanced and respectful understanding of their faith.

The impact of these efforts is profound. By addressing misconceptions and biases, Christians can foster a more inclusive and respectful society. Educational campaigns and public awareness programs provide accurate information and challenge harmful stereotypes. Interfaith dialogues create opportunities for mutual understanding and cooperation. Outreach programs and community service projects demonstrate the practical implications of Christian ethics, showcasing the positive contributions of the faith to society. Christian organizations play a pivotal role in these efforts, organizing initiatives that promote positive engagement and address misconceptions. Through these multifaceted approaches, Christians can contribute to a more accurate and respectful understanding of their faith, fostering a more inclusive and harmonious society.

BUILDING BRIDGES: SUCCESSFUL INTERFAITH PROJECTS

One cannot overstate the profound impact of interfaith projects in bridging divides and fostering understanding among diverse religious communities. Consider the Interfaith Youth Core (IFYC), an organization dedicated to bringing together young people from various faith traditions to engage in dialogue and collaborative action. Founded by Eboo Patel, IFYC has implemented numerous programs that focus on leadership training, service projects, and campus interfaith initiatives. These programs empower young leaders to transcend religious boundaries, promoting mutual respect and cooperation. One notable initiative is their "Better Together" campaign, which encourages college students to work on service projects addressing social issues such as hunger, homelessness, and environmental sustainability. By uniting individuals around common goals, IFYC demonstrates how interfaith collaboration can address pressing societal needs while fostering a sense of shared purpose.

Similarly, the Parliament of the World's Religions exemplifies the transformative power of global interfaith initiatives. Since its first convening in 1893, the Parliament has brought together religious leaders, scholars, and activists from around the world to engage in dialogue and collaborative action. Their global initiatives, such as the "Climate Action Task Force," focus on addressing critical issues like climate change through the lens of faith. By leveraging the moral and ethical teachings of diverse religions, the Parliament fosters a collective commitment to environmental stewardship. These efforts underscore the importance of inclusive and respectful dialogue, as participants are encouraged to share their perspectives and learn from one another, fostering a deeper understanding of the interconnectedness of faith and global challenges.

The success of these interfaith projects is not coincidental but the result of carefully designed elements that make them effective. Inclusive and respectful dialogue is paramount, as it ensures that all voices are heard and valued. This approach fosters an environment of mutual respect and trust, allowing participants to engage in meaningful conversations without fear of judgment or exclusion. Collaboration on common goals and shared values further enhances the effectiveness of these initiatives. By focusing on issues that resonate across religious boundaries, such as social justice, environmental sustainability, and community service, interfaith projects create a sense of unity and collective purpose.

The role of leadership in driving interfaith collaboration cannot be overstated. Effective leaders inspire trust, foster inclusivity, and create a vision that unites diverse groups around common goals. Influential interfaith leaders, such as Eboo Patel, founder of IFYC, and Karen Armstrong, a prominent religious scholar and founder of the Charter for Compassion, have demonstrated the power of visionary leadership in promoting interfaith understanding. Leadership training programs for interfaith initiatives, such as those offered by IFYC, equip emerging leaders with the skills and knowledge necessary to navigate the complexities of interfaith work. These programs emphasize the importance of empathy, active listening, conflict resolution, and collaboration, ensuring that leaders are well-prepared to foster inclusive and respectful dialogue.

The long-term outcomes of interfaith projects for communities are both profound and far-reaching. Data and case studies reveal significant improvements in interfaith relations and community cohesion. Participants often report a greater appreciation for religious diversity and a willingness to engage with individuals from different faith backgrounds. For example, a longitudinal study of IFYC's campus programs found that students who participated in interfaith initiatives displayed higher levels of social cohesion and lower levels of religious prejudice compared to their peers. This enhanced community cooperation is not limited to the duration of the projects but extends into long-term partnerships and collaborative efforts. Communities that have engaged in interfaith dialogue often continue to work together on various initiatives, creating a network of support and collaboration that strengthens the social fabric.

As we reflect on the transformative potential of successful interfaith projects, it becomes evident that building bridges across religious divides is not only possible but essential for fostering a more inclusive and harmonious society. The key elements of these initiatives —inclusive dialogue, collaboration on common goals, and effective leadership—serve as a blueprint for future efforts. The positive outcomes, from improved interfaith relations to sustained community partnerships, underscore the enduring impact of these endeavors. By learning from and building upon these successful examples, we can continue to promote mutual understanding and cooperation, laying the groundwork for a more peaceful and interconnected world.

The next chapter delves into the tangible impacts of secularization on various facets of society, examining how the decline of religious influence shapes our collective moral and ethical landscape.

PRACTICAL APPLICATIONS OF CHRISTIAN TEACHINGS TODAY

Imagine a bustling marketplace in ancient Jerusalem, where merchants haggle over prices and children run through the streets. Amidst the chaos stands a humble man, Jesus of Nazareth, whose teachings on love and compassion would echo through the centuries, shaping the moral frameworks of countless individuals and communities. This chapter explores how the foundational principles of Christian ethics, derived from biblical teachings, can be seamlessly integrated into both personal and professional life, offering a moral compass in an increasingly complex world.

CHRISTIAN ETHICS IN PERSONAL AND PROFESSIONAL LIFE

Christian ethics are rooted in the divine revelations of Scripture, offering a robust framework for moral conduct. The Ten Commandments, given to Moses on Mount Sinai, serve as a foundational moral code. They encompass directives such as "Thou shalt not steal" and "Thou shalt not bear false witness against thy neighbor," which emphasize honesty and integrity. These commandments are not merely ancient edicts but timeless principles that guide ethical behavior. Jesus' teachings further expand on these principles, particularly His emphasis on love and compassion. In the Sermon on the Mount, He exhorts us to love our enemies and pray for those who persecute us, underscoring the transformative power of unconditional love. Paul's letters, rich with ethical guidance, offer practical advice on living a life that reflects the teachings of Christ. In his epistles, Paul advocates for humility, urging believers to consider others more significant than themselves and to serve one another in love.

Applying these ethical teachings in personal life involves a conscious commitment to embodying these principles daily. Practicing honesty and integrity in relationships means being truthful in our interactions, upholding promises, and acting with transparency. Demonstrating kindness and forgiveness, as Jesus taught, involves showing compassion to others, even when it is challenging, and letting go of grudges. Leading a life of humility and service requires a willingness to put others' needs above our own, recognizing that true greatness lies in serving others. These practices not only enrich our personal lives but also build a foundation of trust and respect in our communities.

In professional settings, integrating Christian ethics can be both challenging and rewarding. Ethical decision-making based on Christian values involves considering the moral implications of our actions and striving to align them with biblical principles. For instance, a business leader faced with a decision that could harm the environment might recall the biblical mandate to steward God's creation responsibly. Fair treatment of colleagues and employees is another critical aspect, reflecting the Golden Rule: "Do unto others as you would have them do unto you." This principle encourages treating everyone with respect and dignity, fostering a positive and supportive work environment. Balancing ambition with humility involves recognizing that success is not solely measured by personal achievements but also by the positive impact we have on others. It requires a commitment to ethical practices, even when they may not yield immediate financial gains.

Maintaining Christian ethics in a secular workplace presents unique challenges. Ethical dilemmas often arise, requiring us to navigate complex situations where the right course of action may not be immediately clear. For example, an employee might face pressure to engage in dishonest practices to meet targets, challenging their commitment to integrity. Building a reputation for integrity and trustworthiness in such environments requires consistent adherence to ethical principles, even when it is difficult. This steadfastness can lead to long-term rewards, including the trust and respect of colleagues and superiors. The impact on career advancement and workplace relationships is significant; individuals known for their ethical conduct often become sought-after leaders and mentors, valued for their moral clarity and reliability.

Reflection Section

1. **Reflect on a recent situation where you faced an ethical dilemma at work. How did you resolve it?**
   - Consider the principles you relied on and the outcome of your decision. How did this experience shape your understanding of Christian ethics in the workplace?
2. **Identify areas in your personal life where you can more fully embody Christian ethics.**
   - Think about relationships where honesty, kindness, or forgiveness can be more actively practiced. What steps can you take to integrate these principles more deeply?

3. **Examine your professional environment for opportunities to apply Christian ethics.**
    - Look for ways to promote fairness, respect, and integrity in your interactions with colleagues. How can you balance ambition with humility in your career goals?

By reflecting on these questions, you can gain deeper insights into how Christian ethics can be practically applied in both personal and professional contexts, enriching your life and the lives of those around you.

FAITH-BASED APPROACHES TO SOCIAL JUSTICE

The biblical foundation for social justice is robust, rooted in the ancient calls of the prophets and the teachings of Jesus Christ. The prophets, from Isaiah to Amos, were unrelenting in their calls for justice and mercy. They admonished the Israelites to care for the widow, the orphan, and the stranger, emphasizing that true worship of God necessitated a commitment to social equity. Isaiah's proclamation, "Learn to do right; seek justice. Defend the oppressed. Take up the cause of the fatherless; plead the case of the widow" (Isaiah 1:17), serves as a clarion call to believers, urging them to embody God's justice in their communities. Similarly, Amos's exhortation, "But let justice roll on like a river, righteousness like a never-failing stream!" (Amos 5:24), underscores the inseparability of faith and justice.

Jesus' ministry further amplifies this emphasis on caring for the marginalized. His parables and actions consistently highlighted the importance of serving the poor, the sick, and the outcast. The Parable of the Good Samaritan is a quintessential example, illustrating the imperative to love and care for one's neighbor, regardless of social or ethnic boundaries. Jesus' Beatitudes, particularly "Blessed are the merciful, for they shall receive mercy" (Matthew 5:7) and "Blessed are those who hunger and thirst for righteousness, for they shall be filled" (Matthew 5:6), encapsulate His vision of a just and compassionate society. The New Testament epistles, especially those of Paul and James, provide additional instructions on equitable treatment. Paul's letters often address the need for fairness and equality within the Christian community, advocating for the dismantling of social hierarchies in favor of unity in Christ. James, in his epistle, warns against favoritism and emphasizes the importance of caring for the poor, stating, "Religion that God our Father accepts as pure and faultless is this: to look after orphans and widows in their distress" (James 1:27).

Historically, faith-based social justice movements have left indelible marks on society. The abolitionist movement, driven by Christian activists, sought to eradicate the moral blight of slavery. Figures like William Wilberforce in Britain and Harriet Beecher Stowe in America leveraged their faith to rally against the dehumanization inherent in slavery. Wilberforce, inspired by his evangelical convictions, dedicated his life to the abolition of the transatlantic slave trade, while Stowe's novel, "Uncle Tom's Cabin," galvanized public opinion by depicting the brutal realities of slavery. Similarly, the Civil Rights Movement in the United States saw churches at the forefront of the struggle for racial equality. Dr. Martin Luther King Jr., a Baptist minister, harnessed biblical principles to advocate for nonviolent resistance against segregation and discrimination. His iconic "I Have a Dream" speech is suffused with biblical references, framing the quest for civil rights as a divine mandate for justice and equality.

Engaging in social justice today requires actionable steps rooted in faith. Volunteering with faith-based organizations is a tangible way to make a difference. These organizations often address a myriad of issues, from homelessness to food insecurity, providing opportunities for hands-on service. Advocating for policy changes based on Christian principles involves participating in the democratic process, whether through voting, lobbying, or engaging in public discourse. Supporting initiatives that address poverty and inequality can also include financial contributions to causes that align with Christian values, as well as active participation in community projects aimed at uplifting the marginalized.

The challenges of faith-based social justice work are manifold. Balancing activism with personal faith can be taxing, requiring a constant renewal of spiritual strength through prayer and reflection. Building coalitions with secular organizations, while beneficial for broader impact, can entail navigating differing worldviews and priorities. Nevertheless, the rewards are profound. Serving others in the name of faith can lead to spiritual fulfillment, fostering a deeper connection with God and a greater sense of purpose. The act of serving, grounded in the teachings of Christ, not only transforms the lives of those helped but also enriches the soul of the servant, creating a ripple effect of compassion and justice.

INTEGRATING FAITH WITH MODERN CAREER GOALS

In the frenetic pace of modern life, the alignment of career goals with Christian values often feels like navigating a labyrinth. Yet, this alignment is crucial, offering both moral clarity and a sense of purpose. Choosing professions that resonate with ethical principles is a foundational step. Imagine a young professional, fresh out of university, faced with the choice between a lucrative job at a firm known for its questionable practices and a modestly paying role in a non-profit dedicated to social justice. The decision becomes clear when viewed through the lens of faith, prioritizing integrity and service over financial gain. This approach requires discernment and a willingness to sometimes forgo immediate rewards for long-term fulfillment.

Setting career goals that reflect Christian priorities involves more than just selecting the right profession; it demands a holistic vision of one's life and work. Goals should not merely focus on personal advancement but also consider how one's skills and talents can serve the greater good. For instance, a medical professional might aim not only to excel in their field but also to provide care to under-served communities, embodying the Christian call to heal and serve. This broader perspective transforms career aspirations into a voca-tion, a calling that transcends the mundane pursuit of success.

Understanding vocation as a calling from God adds depth to career decisions. Vocation, derived from the Latin "vocare," meaning "to call," signifies a divine invitation to use one's gifts in service to others. This concept is not limited to religious vocations but extends to all professions. The process of discernment, crucial in identifying one's calling, involves prayer, reflection, and seeking counsel from trusted advisors. It is a journey of listening to God's voice in the quiet moments of life and recognizing the passions and talents He has bestowed. This spiritual practice ensures that career choices are not merely pragmatic but deeply rooted in one's faith and purpose.

Integrating faith with daily work requires intentional practices that keep one grounded and spiritually nourished. Establishing a work-life-faith balance is paramount. This balance is not about rigid compartmentalization but about creating a harmonious rhythm where work, rest, and spiritual practices coexist. Creating moments for prayer and reflection during the workday can be as simple as taking a few minutes to meditate on a scripture passage or offering a silent prayer for guidance before a meeting. These practices infuse the workday with a sense of divine presence, reminding individuals that their work is an extension of their worship.

The impact of faith on career satisfaction and success is profound. When work is perceived as a vocation, it imbues everyday tasks with meaning and purpose, leading to increased job satisfaction. This sense of fulfillment is not dependent on external accolades but on the internal conviction that one's work aligns with God's will. Enhanced relationships with colleagues often follow, as ethical behavior and genuine care for others foster a positive and collaborative work environment. Trust and respect, earned through consistent ethical conduct, pave the way for deeper connections and mutual support.

Personal fulfillment from aligning work with faith transcends the professional sphere, spilling over into all areas of life. It nurtures a sense of coherence and integrity, where actions and beliefs are in harmony. This alignment provides a resilient foundation, enabling individuals to navigate challenges and ethical dilemmas with confidence and grace. Moreover, it offers a profound sense of peace, knowing that one's efforts are contributing to a greater good and reflecting the love of Christ in the world.

In the labyrinth of modern career paths, integrating faith with professional aspirations is not merely an option but a profound calling. It demands intentionality, discernment, and a commitment to living out Christian values in every aspect of one's work. This integration transforms careers into vocations, imbuing them with purpose and aligning them with God's divine plan. Through this alignment, work becomes a sacred act, a testament to one's faith, and a beacon of light in the corporate world.

PRACTICAL SPIRITUAL PRACTICES FOR DAILY LIFE

The importance of daily spiritual practices cannot be overstated, for they serve as the bedrock of a robust and resilient faith life. These practices, when integrated into the rhythm of daily existence, facilitate a deeper connection with the Divine, offering spiritual nourishment and guidance. Prayer, often described as a daily conversation with God, is fundamental. It is not merely a ritual but an intimate dialogue where one can express gratitude, seek forgiveness, and request divine intervention. This practice fosters a sense of closeness to God, transforming the mundane into the sacred. Bible reading and meditation are equally vital, providing spiritual sustenance and wisdom. The Scriptures, rich with divine revelations, offer insights into God's character and His will for humanity. Meditating on these texts allows for a profound internalization of their teachings, enabling believers to align their lives with biblical principles. Participation in communal worship, whether in a traditional church setting or a small group, reinforces these individual practices, fostering a sense of community and shared purpose. Gathering with fellow believers to sing hymns, pray, and hear the Word preached creates a collective spiritual energy, strengthening individual faith through communal support.

Different forms of prayer offer varied benefits, catering to the diverse spiritual needs of individuals. Intercessory prayer, where one prays on behalf of others, embodies the Christian call to love and serve. It cultivates empathy, reinforcing the interconnectedness of the faith community. By lifting others in prayer, believers participate in the divine work of healing and restoration, often witnessing the power of collective supplication. Contemplative prayer, on the other hand, is a practice of stillness and reflection, seeking inner peace and divine presence. It is an exercise in quieting the mind and opening the heart to God's voice, fostering a deep sense of tranquility and spiritual clarity. Praying the Psalms, an ancient practice, provides both guidance and comfort. These poetic prayers, rich with emotion and theological depth, articulate the full range of human experience, from lamentation to exaltation. They offer a structured yet intimate way to converse with God, grounding the believer in scriptural truths while addressing personal and communal concerns.

Incorporating these spiritual practices into daily routines requires intentionality and discipline. Setting aside specific times for prayer and reflection, whether in the morning, during a lunch break, or before bed, ensures that these practices become habitual. Consistency is key, as regular engagement fosters a deeper and more sustained spiritual connection. Creating a dedicated space for spiritual activities can also enhance the practice. This space, whether a quiet corner of a room or a small altar, serves as a physical reminder of one's commitment to spiritual growth. It can be adorned with symbols of faith, such as a cross, a Bible, or candles, creating an environment conducive to contemplation and prayer. This sacred space becomes a sanctuary in the midst of daily chaos, offering a refuge where one can retreat to commune with God.

Maintaining daily spiritual practices, however, is not without its challenges. In our fast-paced, distraction-laden world, finding time for quiet reflection can be daunting. Overcoming these distractions requires a conscious effort to prioritize spiritual growth, often necessitating the elimination of less essential activities. Time constraints, particularly for those juggling work, family, and other responsibilities, can also pose significant obstacles. Yet, even brief moments of prayer or meditation can be profoundly impactful, serving as a spiritual anchor throughout the day. The benefits of maintaining these practices are manifold. They facilitate spiritual growth, deepening one's understanding of God's character and will. Regular engagement in prayer and meditation fosters a deeper connection with God, imbuing daily life with a sense of divine purpose and guidance. This connection provides a source of comfort and strength, enabling believers to navigate life's challenges with grace and resilience.

These daily spiritual practices serve as the lifeblood of a vibrant faith, offering nourishment and sustenance for the soul. They transform the ordinary into the extraordinary, infusing everyday life with divine presence and purpose.

APPLYING BIBLICAL TEACHINGS TO CONTEMPORARY ISSUES

Consider the relevance of biblical teachings as they guide us through the labyrinth of modern issues, offering timeless wisdom for contemporary decision-making. Biblical principles on stewardship and environmental care, for instance, are profoundly instructive. Genesis 2:15 reminds us that humanity is tasked with "working and keeping" the Garden of Eden, a mandate that extends to our stewardship of the Earth today. This principle emphasizes the responsible use of resources, advocating for sustainable practices that ensure the well-being of future generations. Similarly, teachings on justice and equality permeate the Bible, with scriptures like Micah 6:8 calling us to "act justly, love mercy, and walk humbly with our God." These teachings guide social policies, urging us to create equitable systems that uplift the marginalized and oppressed. Ethical business practices are also addressed, with Proverbs 11:1 declaring, "The Lord detests dishonest scales, but accurate weights find favor with him," underscoring the importance of honesty and integrity in commerce.

In examining specific contemporary issues through the lens of scripture, the imperative of environmental stewardship stands out. Climate change, a pressing global concern, demands an urgent and faith-informed response. The biblical call to stewardship compels us to adopt sustainable practices, reduce our carbon footprint, and advocate for policies that protect God's creation. Economic inequality, another critical issue, can be addressed through the biblical emphasis on justice and equity. Scriptures like James 2:15-16 challenge us to provide for those in need, urging us to support policies that promote fair wages, access to education, and healthcare. Technology, with its rapid advancements, presents ethical considerations that can be navigated through biblical teachings. The wisdom of 1 Corinthians 6:12, "I have the right to do anything—but not everything is beneficial," guides us in making ethical choices in technology use, balancing innovation with responsibility and empathy.

To apply these biblical teachings to contemporary issues, one must take actionable steps rooted in faith. Engaging in sustainable practices based on stewardship principles involves simple yet impactful actions, such as reducing waste, conserving energy, and supporting eco-friendly products. These daily choices reflect a commitment to caring for God's creation. Advocating for policies that promote justice and equality requires active participation in the democratic process. This can include voting for leaders who prioritize social justice, contacting representatives to voice support for equitable policies, and participating in community advocacy groups. Making ethical choices in technology use involves being mindful of privacy concerns, avoiding harmful online behavior, and supporting tech companies that prioritize ethical practices.

Applying biblical teachings in modern contexts is not without challenges. Navigating conflicts between faith and societal norms can be daunting. For example, advocating for environmental policies might clash with economic interests, requiring a delicate balance of ethical considerations. However, the rewards of living out biblical principles are profound. Experiencing spiritual fulfillment from aligning actions with faith provides a deep sense of purpose and connection to God's will. This alignment fosters resilience and inner peace, empowering individuals to face contemporary challenges with unwavering faith.

The relevance of biblical teachings in addressing modern issues highlights their timeless wisdom and practical applicability. By grounding our actions in these principles, we navigate the complexities of contemporary life with integrity and compassion. The challenges we face today, from climate change to economic inequality, call for a faith-informed response that reflects the justice, stewardship, and ethical conduct taught in the Bible.

In the next chapter, we will delve into the dynamics of navigating religious doubts and strengthening faith, exploring how to maintain spiritual resilience in an ever-changing world. This exploration will offer insights into overcoming challenges and deepening one's faith journey, providing practical guidance for a more robust spiritual life.

NAVIGATING RELIGIOUS DOUBTS AND STRENGTHENING FAITH

In a world increasingly characterized by rapid technological advancements and shifting cultural norms, the question of faith remains a bedrock issue for many. Consider the story of a young seminarian, well-versed in theology and deeply committed to his vocation, who finds himself grappling with profound existential questions triggered by the sudden loss of a loved one. This scenario, while deeply personal, is emblematic of the broader phenomenon of religious doubt—a phenomenon that is neither new nor uncommon but one that continues to challenge believers across the spectrum of age and expertise.

UNDERSTANDING AND NAVIGATING RELIGIOUS DOUBTS

Religious doubt, in its multifaceted nature, often emerges from a confluence of intellectual challenges and existential crises. On an intellectual level, questions about the veracity of sacred texts, the problem of evil, and the apparent conflict between science and religion can serve as significant catalysts for doubt. These challenges are not merely academic but strike at the very core of one's belief system, demanding rigorous scrutiny and often leading to a reevaluation of long-held convictions. Moreover, personal crises—such as the death of a loved one, serious illness, or other forms of suffering—can precipitate a crisis of faith, compelling individuals to question the benevolence and omnipotence of God. These moments of suffering often bring to the forefront theodicy, or the justification of divine goodness in the face of evil, a question that has perplexed theologians and laypersons alike for centuries.

Negative experiences with religious institutions or leaders further compound these doubts. Instances of hypocrisy, moral failings, or abuse within religious communities can profoundly shake one's faith. When the very institutions that are supposed to embody divine principles falter, it can lead to a disillusionment that extends beyond the institution itself, casting a shadow over the faith it represents. Cultural and societal influences also play a pivotal role in shaping religious doubt. In a secular world where religious beliefs are increasingly questioned and sometimes ridiculed, maintaining one's faith can become an uphill battle. The pervasive ethos of skepticism, fueled by media portrayals and academic discourse, often challenges the plausibility of religious beliefs, leading individuals to grapple with their convictions.

The psychological and emotional dimensions of doubt are equally significant. Feelings of guilt and shame often accompany religious doubts, particularly in communities where unwavering faith is valorized. The internal conflict between doubt and belief can engender anxiety and fear as individuals grapple with the implications of their uncertainty. This emotional turmoil is not merely a byproduct of doubt but a central aspect of the experience, affecting one's sense of identity and purpose. The existential weight of these questions can lead to a profound sense of isolation, as individuals may feel alienated from their faith communities and even from themselves.

Theologically, doubt occupies a nuanced position within Christian thought. Far from being an aberration, doubt is often seen as an integral part of the faith experience. St. Augustine's notion of "faith seeking understanding" encapsulates this perspective, viewing doubt not as a failure of faith but as a catalyst for deeper inquiry and understanding. Similarly, St. Thomas Aquinas, while positing that faith and doubt are fundamentally incompatible, acknowledges that the process of wrestling with doubt can lead to a more robust and mature faith. Contemporary theologians have built on these foundations, emphasizing the constructive potential of doubt. They argue that doubt can serve as a refining fire, stripping away superficial beliefs and leading to a more authentic and resilient faith.

Navigating through periods of doubt requires practical and intentional strategies. Seeking guidance from trusted spiritual mentors can provide invaluable support and perspective. These mentors, often seasoned in their own faith journeys, can offer wisdom and reassurance, helping to contextualize doubts within the broader tapestry of spiritual growth. Engaging in reflective practices such as journaling allows individuals to articulate their doubts and explore them in a safe and structured manner. This process of externalizing internal struggles can lead to greater clarity and insight, transforming nebulous fears into concrete questions that can be addressed.

Participating in open and honest dialogues about faith can also be profoundly therapeutic. Whether within small groups, faith communities, or interfaith forums, these discussions provide a platform for individuals to voice their doubts and receive feedback from others who may have faced similar challenges. The communal aspect of these dialogues fosters a sense of solidarity and shared purpose, mitigating the isolation that often accompanies doubt. Such conversations can reveal the universality of doubt, reinforcing the notion that questioning is a natural and even necessary aspect of a vibrant and dynamic faith.

Reflection Section: Journaling Prompts

- Reflect on a moment of personal crisis that led you to question your faith. What specific questions or doubts arose, and how did you initially respond to them?
- Consider a time when intellectual challenges caused you to doubt your beliefs. What resources (books, mentors, discussions) helped you navigate these doubts?
- Write about an experience where a negative encounter with a religious institution or leader impacted your faith. How did you cope with this disillusionment, and what steps did you take to rebuild your trust?
- Explore the cultural and societal influences that have shaped your faith journey. In what ways have these influences either strengthened or weakened your beliefs?
- Reflect on the emotional aspects of your doubts. How have feelings of guilt, shame, or anxiety affected your relationship with your faith community and with God?
- Consider the theological perspectives on doubt that resonate with you. How can these perspectives help you reframe your doubts as opportunities for growth rather than obstacles to faith?

In navigating religious doubts, it is crucial to acknowledge the complexity and multifaceted nature of the experience. By understanding the intellectual, emotional, and theological dimensions of doubt and by employing practical strategies to address these challenges, individuals can transform periods of uncertainty into opportunities for deeper faith and understanding.

STRATEGIES FOR STRENGTHENING PERSONAL FAITH

Regular spiritual practices serve as the bedrock of a robust and resilient faith. The discipline of daily prayer and meditation creates a sacred space for communion with the divine, allowing you to center your thoughts and find tranquility amidst life's chaos. This daily ritual, while seemingly simple, can profoundly transform your spiritual landscape, fostering a deeper connection with God. Similarly, regular participation in worship services anchors you within a community of believers, offering not only spiritual nourishment but also a sense of belonging and shared purpose. The act of congregating, singing hymns, and partaking in communal prayers weaves a tapestry of faith that is both personal and collective. Engaging in spiritual reading and study further enriches this tapestry, providing intellectual and theological insights that deepen your understanding of sacred texts and doctrines.

To deepen your personal faith, setting spiritual goals and tracking your progress can be immensely beneficial. These goals might include committing to regular prayer, reading specific religious texts, or participating in community service. Tracking your progress not only provides a sense of accomplishment but also highlights areas that need more attention, allowing you to adjust your practices accordingly. Creating a personal retreat for focused spiritual reflection can offer a rejuvenating break from the demands of daily life. Whether it's a weekend getaway or a day spent in quiet contemplation, these retreats provide an opportunity to reconnect with your faith on a deeper level. Engaging in acts of service and charity is another powerful way to express and strengthen your faith. By serving others, you embody the teachings of Christ, demonstrating love and compassion in tangible ways. These acts of kindness not only benefit those you serve but also reinforce your own spiritual convictions, making your faith an active and dynamic force in the world.

Religious education plays a crucial role in fortifying faith, offering both formal and informal avenues for growth. Attending Bible study groups and theological courses provides structured learning environments where you can delve into the complexities of scripture and doctrine. These settings foster intellectual engagement and offer opportunities for discussion and debate, enriching your understanding of your faith. Reading works by influential Christian authors, such as C.S. Lewis, Dietrich Bonhoeffer, or Henri Nouwen, can provide profound insights and inspiration. These authors grappled with their own questions and doubts, and their writings often offer solace and guidance. Exploring online courses and resources on faith can also be incredibly enriching. Platforms like Coursera and The Great Courses offer a wide range of religious studies courses, allowing you to learn at your own pace and tailor your education to your specific interests.

Personal experiences and encounters with God form the cornerstone of a living faith. Reflecting on moments of divine intervention or inspiration can provide a wellspring of strength and reassurance. These experiences, whether they are dramatic epiphanies or quiet moments of clarity, serve as touchstones that reaffirm your belief in the presence and power of God. Sharing personal testimonies within faith communities can also be profoundly impactful. These stories not only strengthen your own faith but also inspire and encourage others, creating a ripple effect of spiritual renewal. Recognizing and appreciating everyday miracles and blessings is another way to cultivate a grateful and faith-filled heart. The simple acts of acknowledging the beauty of a sunrise, the joy of a child's laughter, or the kindness of a stranger can transform your perspective, helping you to see the divine in the mundane.

Reflection Section: Setting Spiritual Goals

- Identify three specific spiritual goals you would like to achieve in the next six months. These could include practices such as daily prayer, attending a Bible study group, or volunteering with a charitable organization.
- Write down actionable steps you can take to achieve each goal. Consider what resources or support you might need and how you will track your progress.
- Reflect on any potential obstacles you might face in achieving these goals and brainstorm strategies to overcome them. This could involve setting aside specific times for prayer, finding a study partner, or scheduling regular check-ins with a spiritual mentor.
- At the end of each month, review your progress and reflect on what you have learned. Adjust your goals and steps as needed to ensure that you continue to grow in your faith.

By incorporating these strategies into your daily life, you can cultivate a faith that is both deeply personal and communally enriched. The practices of prayer, meditation, worship, and study, combined with acts of service and continuous learning, create a holistic approach to spiritual growth. Personal experiences and encounters with the divine further reinforce this growth, transforming your faith into a lived reality that permeates every aspect of your life.

THE ROLE OF COMMUNITY IN ADDRESSING DOUBTS

Religious communities serve as sanctuaries of support and understanding during times of doubt, providing invaluable spaces where individuals can express their uncertainties without fear of judgment. Within the sanctuary of communal faith, you find an environment that encourages open discussions, where questions are not only welcomed but seen as integral to spiritual growth. Such spaces are essential for emotional and spiritual support, offering a network of individuals who can empathize with your struggles and provide both solace and encouragement. This collective support system fosters a sense of accountability and mutual growth, helping you navigate the tumultuous waters of doubt with the assurance that you are not alone in your journey.

The benefits of smaller, more intimate groups within these larger communities cannot be overstated. These small groups, often formed around specific interests or life stages, allow for the development of deeper relationships and trust. In these settings, personalized support and guidance become possible, as members can share their experiences and insights in a more focused and meaningful way. These groups also create opportunities for shared spiritual practices, such as group prayer, Bible study, and worship, which can reinforce faith and provide a sense of belonging. The intimacy of these gatherings fosters a safe environment where you can explore your doubts and fears with others who are equally committed to seeking truth and understanding.

Several community initiatives have proven effective in addressing doubts and fostering spiritual growth. Support groups specifically tailored for individuals struggling with faith provide a dedicated space for discussing doubts and exploring potential resolutions. These groups often employ structured discussions and guided reflections to help members articulate their concerns and find pathways forward. Community retreats focused on spiritual renewal offer a respite from the daily grind, allowing for deep reflection and rejuvenation. These retreats often include workshops, prayer sessions, and meditative practices designed to facilitate a reconnection with faith. Mentorship programs linking experienced believers with those in doubt provide a one-on-one support system that can be incredibly impactful. These mentors, having navigated their own periods of doubt, can offer wisdom, perspective, and encouragement, helping mentees to find their footing and continue their spiritual journey with renewed vigor.

The role of communal worship and shared rituals in strengthening individual faith is profound. Participating in communal prayer and worship services creates a collective energy that can be deeply uplifting and affirming. These shared experiences remind you that faith is not a solitary endeavor but a communal one, sustained by the collective devotion and support of the community. Celebrating religious festivals and traditions together reinforces a sense of continuity and shared heritage, grounding you in the rich history and practices of your faith. These celebrations, filled with symbolic rituals and communal activities, serve as powerful reminders of the enduring truths of your beliefs. Engaging in communal acts of service and charity further solidifies this sense of shared purpose. By working together to serve others, you not only embody the teachings of your faith but also strengthen the bonds within the community, creating a network of support that can sustain you through periods of doubt and uncertainty.

These various aspects of community life—open discussions, personalized support, communal worship, and shared service—collectively create a robust framework for addressing doubts and fostering spiritual growth. They provide not only the intellectual and emotional support needed to navigate times of uncertainty but also the practical guidance and communal encouragement essential for sustaining faith in the long term.

FINDING RELEVANCE IN ANCIENT TEXTS

In the quiet solitude of a late evening, you might find yourself opening a well-worn Bible, the pages yellowed with age and the margins filled with notes from years gone by. The ancient words inscribed within hold a timeless wisdom that transcends the centuries, offering moral and ethical teachings that remain profoundly relevant. The scriptures, with their narratives of human struggle, redemption, and divine interaction, provide a moral compass applicable to the complexities of modern life. Consider the Sermon on the Mount, where Jesus' teachings on humility, mercy, and justice resonate just as powerfully today as they did two millennia ago. These principles offer a framework for ethical behavior that can guide decisions in both personal and professional spheres, encouraging actions rooted in compassion and integrity.

The stories and parables found within these sacred texts offer timeless lessons that speak to the human condition. Take, for instance, the parable of the Good Samaritan. This narrative transcends its historical context, illustrating the universal principle of loving and aiding one's neighbor, irrespective of cultural or religious differences. Such stories, rich in metaphor and moral teaching, provide profound insights into the nature of human relationships and societal obligations. The prophetic insights scattered throughout the scriptures, from Isaiah's calls for social justice to Jeremiah's laments over societal decay, offer incisive commentaries on human nature and society. These prophetic voices challenge readers to reflect on contemporary issues through the lens of divine justice and righteousness, urging a commitment to ethical living and social responsibility.

Interpreting these ancient texts in contemporary contexts requires thoughtful and deliberate methods. Contextual Bible study methods, which consider the historical, cultural, and linguistic background of the scriptures, allow for a deeper understanding of their original intent and significance. By comparing historical interpretations with modern perspectives, you can uncover new layers of meaning that resonate with current issues. For example, examining the historical context of the Beatitudes can shed light on their revolutionary nature, while modern interpretations can apply their principles to contemporary social justice movements. Applying scriptural principles to current issues, such as environmental stewardship or economic inequality, can provide a moral framework for addressing these challenges, rooted in the timeless wisdom of the scriptures.

Scholarly resources and commentaries play a crucial role in this interpretative process, offering academic insights that enhance your understanding of ancient texts. Theological commentaries and study guides provide detailed explanations and analyses of biblical passages, drawing on historical-critical methods to uncover the nuances of the text. Engaging with contemporary theological scholarship allows you to explore diverse perspectives and interpretations, enriching your understanding and appreciation of the scriptures. This scholarly engagement fosters a dynamic and evolving relationship with the texts, encouraging continuous learning and reflection.

Integrating the ancient wisdom of scriptures into daily life involves practical and intentional steps. Creating a daily scripture reading and reflection plan can establish a routine that fosters spiritual growth and moral clarity. This practice, whether undertaken in the quiet moments of the morning or the reflective hours of the evening, allows you to internalize the teachings and principles of the scriptures. Writing personal reflections and applications of scripture further deepens this engagement, as the act of writing helps to crystallize your thoughts and insights. These reflections can serve as a personal journal of your spiritual journey, documenting your growth and understanding over time.

Discussing scriptural insights with family and friends provides an opportunity for communal learning and support. These conversations, whether around the dinner table or in a Bible study group, allow for the sharing of perspectives and experiences, enriching your understanding of the texts. The communal aspect of these discussions fosters a sense of shared purpose and collective growth, reinforcing the principles and teachings of the scriptures within a supportive and nurturing environment. This communal engagement with the scriptures transforms them from ancient texts into living documents that shape and guide your daily life, providing a moral and spiritual foundation that endures through the ages.

PERSONAL TESTIMONIES: STORIES OF FAITH AND DOUBT

Consider the life of Mother Teresa, who is widely revered as a paragon of Christian virtue and compassion. Yet, her private letters, published posthumously, reveal a profound and enduring struggle with spiritual darkness and doubt. For nearly fifty years, she experienced what she described as a "terrible dryness" and a sense of the absence of God. Despite this internal turmoil, she continued her mission, serving the poorest of the poor with unwavering dedication. Her testimony provides a poignant example of how faith can persist amidst doubt and how acts of love and service can be sustained even when spiritual consolation is elusive.

Equally compelling are the stories of everyday believers who have navigated their own periods of doubt. Take, for instance, the account of a nurse named Sarah, who found herself questioning God's goodness after witnessing the suffering of her patients during a particularly harrowing month in the intensive care unit. Overwhelmed by the apparent senselessness of the pain she encountered daily, Sarah began to doubt the existence of a benevolent deity. However, through conversations with a hospital chaplain and participation in a support group for healthcare workers, she found a renewed sense of purpose and faith. These dialogues allowed her to reconcile her doubts with her vocation, ultimately viewing her work as a manifestation of God's love and compassion in a broken world.

The transformative power of personal testimonies lies in their ability to bridge the gap between abstract theological concepts and lived human experience. When individuals share their stories of doubt and faith, they offer a unique form of encouragement that resonates deeply with others facing similar struggles. These narratives foster a sense of empathy and understanding within communities, breaking down the barriers of isolation that often accompany doubt. As listeners hear these stories, they gain a renewed perspective on their own experiences, realizing that doubt is not an anomaly but a common aspect of the faith experience. This shared understanding can lead to a collective strengthening of faith as individuals find solace in knowing they are not alone in their struggles.

Sharing personal faith stories requires a focus on authenticity and honesty. It is crucial to present your experiences without embellishment or omission, as genuine accounts are far more impactful than those that seem contrived. Highlighting moments of divine intervention or guidance can illustrate how faith has been a sustaining force in your life, even during times of uncertainty. Emphasizing the lessons learned and the growth experienced through these challenges can provide valuable insights for others navigating similar paths. By being transparent about your doubts and the ways in which you have worked through them, you offer a roadmap for others, showing that faith can be resilient and adaptive.

Incorporating personal testimonies into communal worship and study can significantly enhance the spiritual life of a community. Sharing testimonies during worship services provides a powerful witness to the ongoing work of God in the lives of believers. These narratives can inspire and uplift the congregation, reinforcing the relevance of faith in everyday life. Including personal stories in Bible study discussions can deepen the engagement with scripture, as participants relate the biblical teachings to contemporary experiences. This approach fosters a dynamic and interactive learning environment where the ancient texts come alive through the lens of modern life. Creating platforms for sharing experiences within the community, such as testimony nights or faith-sharing groups, can further strengthen the bonds among members, fostering a supportive and nurturing environment where faith can flourish.

As we consider the role of personal testimonies in navigating religious doubts and strengthening faith, it becomes evident that these stories are not merely anecdotal but are integral to the communal and individual dimensions of faith. The authenticity and vulnerability inherent in these narratives create a space for genuine connection and growth, enriching the spiritual journey for both the storyteller and the listener. By sharing our experiences of doubt and faith, we contribute to a collective wisdom that sustains and nurtures the community, reinforcing the belief that faith, even when challenged, remains a powerful and transformative force. This dynamic interplay between personal and communal faith forms the bedrock of a resilient and enduring spiritual life, guiding us through the complexities of modern existence.

By weaving these testimonies into the fabric of communal worship and study, we not only honor the individual experiences of believers but also create a collective narrative that celebrates the multifaceted nature of faith. This shared journey, marked by moments of doubt and revelation, strengthens the bonds within the community, fostering an environment where faith can thrive and grow. As we transition to the next chapter, let us carry forward the insights gained from these personal stories, recognizing the profound impact they have on our understanding of faith and our ability to navigate its challenges.

THE ROLE OF CHRISTIANITY IN ETHICAL AND MORAL ISSUES

Imagine, if you will, the bustling agora of ancient Athens, where Socrates engaged in rigorous debate with his fellow citizens, challenging them to examine their lives and their beliefs. Now, transport yourself to a modern-day boardroom, where executives grapple with decisions that could impact thousands of lives. Whether in the ancient world or today, the quest for ethical clarity remains a central human endeavor. For Christians, this quest is deeply rooted in the teachings of the Bible, which provide a robust framework for addressing contemporary ethical dilemmas.

CHRISTIAN PERSPECTIVES ON MODERN ETHICAL DILEMMAS

The foundation of Christian ethics is firmly established in biblical principles, which offer timeless guidance for navigating the moral complexities of modern life. The Ten Commandments, etched in stone and handed down to Moses, continue to resonate with contemporary relevance. "Thou shalt not steal," for instance, transcends its ancient context to address modern issues of corporate fraud and intellectual property theft. Similarly, "Thou shalt not bear false witness" underlines the importance of truthfulness in a world rife with misinformation and deceit.

Jesus' Sermon on the Mount, delivered on a hillside overlooking the Sea of Galilee, serves as a moral framework that challenges believers to embody virtues such as humility, mercy, and peacemaking. "Blessed are the peacemakers," Jesus proclaimed, "for they shall be called the children of God." This beatitude compels Christians to seek reconciliation and justice in a world often divided by conflict and strife. The Sermon's radical call to love one's enemies and turn the other cheek offers a countercultural ethic that stands in stark contrast to the prevailing norms of retribution and vengeance.

The Apostle Paul's teachings on love and justice further enrich the Christian ethical landscape. In his letter to the Romans, Paul exhorts believers to "let love be genuine," to "hate what is evil," and to "hold fast to what is good." These directives are not mere platitudes but actionable imperatives that guide ethical decision-making. Paul's emphasis on justice, particularly in his epistles to the Corinthians and the Galatians, underscores the necessity of fairness and equity in all dealings, whether personal or professional.

When analyzing specific modern ethical dilemmas through a Christian lens, the principles derived from these teachings provide invaluable insights. Consider the ethics of artificial intelligence and automation. As machines increasingly perform tasks once reserved for humans, questions arise about the displacement of workers and the moral implications of creating machines that can mimic human intelligence. From a Christian perspective, the dignity of work and the inherent value of human beings must be paramount. Ethical AI development should prioritize the welfare of individuals and communities, ensuring that technology serves humanity rather than undermines it.

Genetic engineering and human enhancement present another complex ethical frontier. The possibility of editing genes to eliminate diseases or enhance physical and cognitive abilities raises profound questions about the sanctity of life and the limits of human intervention. Christian ethics, grounded in the belief that humans are created in the image of God, caution against playing God by altering the fundamental aspects of human nature. The potential benefits must be weighed against the risks of unintended consequences and the moral imperative to respect the integrity of creation.

In the realm of business practices, ethical considerations abound. Issues such as fair wages, labor exploitation, and environmental stewardship demand a principled approach. Christian ethics call for honesty, integrity, and the just treatment of all workers. Businesses are urged to consider the broader impact of their operations on society and the environment, aligning their practices with the biblical mandate to "love thy neighbor" and to steward the earth responsibly.

Privacy and data security in the digital age also pose significant ethical challenges. The unprecedented collection and use of personal data by corporations and governments raise concerns about consent, transparency, and the potential for abuse. Christian ethics emphasize the inherent worth and dignity of every individual, advocating for the protection of personal privacy and the responsible handling of information. This perspective calls for robust safeguards and ethical guidelines to ensure data is used in ways that respect individual rights and promote the common good.

The role of the Church in guiding ethical behavior is indispensable. Christian institutions, from local congregations to global denominations, provide moral guidance through teachings and official statements on various ethical issues. The Church's prophetic voice can advocate for justice, challenge systemic injustices, and offer a moral compass in times of ethical uncertainty. Christian education, whether through Sunday school, Bible study groups, or faith-based schools, plays a crucial role in ethical formation, instilling values that guide believers in making principled decisions.

For Christians facing ethical dilemmas, practical steps can help align actions with biblical principles. Seeking counsel from spiritual mentors who can provide wisdom and perspective is invaluable. Engaging in prayer and reflection before making decisions allows for divine guidance and discernment. Participating in ethical discussions within faith communities fosters a supportive environment where complex issues can be navigated collectively, drawing on the shared wisdom and experiences of the community.

Reflect on your own experiences and consider the ethical dilemmas you face in daily life. How do the teachings of the Ten Commandments, the Sermon on the Mount, and the letters of Paul influence your decision-making? Engage with your faith community to discuss these issues, seek wisdom from spiritual mentors, and make time for prayer and reflection as you strive to live out your Christian values in a complex world.

THE ROLE OF FAITH IN BIOETHICAL ISSUES

The intersection of faith and bioethics presents a profound terrain where Christian beliefs illuminate the path through some of the most intricate moral quandaries of our time. Central to this discourse is the sanctity of life, a principle deeply embedded in

Christian doctrine. The belief that life is sacred, as it is bestowed by God, forms the bedrock upon which many bioethical perspectives are constructed. This conviction undergirds the Christian view on human dignity and personhood, asserting that every human being is created in the image of God, imago Dei, and therefore possesses intrinsic worth that must be respected and protected.

Consider the contentious issue of abortion and reproductive technologies. From a Christian perspective, the sanctity of life begins at conception, making abortion morally problematic as it constitutes the taking of innocent human life. This perspective extends to certain reproductive technologies that may involve the destruction of embryos. The ethical implications of in vitro fertilization (IVF), for instance, are scrutinized through the lens of personhood, raising questions about the moral status of unused embryos. Christian ethics urge caution and seek to balance the desire for parenthood with the respect for nascent human life.

End-of-life care and euthanasia present another set of profound ethical dilemmas. Christianity advocates for the sanctity of life until natural death, opposing euthanasia and physician-assisted suicide. This stance is rooted in the belief that life, regardless of its quality or condition, remains sacred. However, this does not preclude the compassionate alleviation of suffering. Palliative care, which aims to provide relief from the symptoms and stress of serious illness, is strongly supported as it aligns with the Christian duty to care for the sick and dying without hastening death.

Stem cell research and cloning further complicate the ethical landscape. Christian ethics support the use of adult stem cells, which do not involve the destruction of embryos, for therapeutic purposes. However, the use of embryonic stem cells, which requires the destruction of embryos, is viewed as morally impermissible.

Cloning, particularly human cloning, is also opposed on the grounds that it undermines the uniqueness of individuals and the natural process of procreation, reflecting a utilitarian approach that treats human life as a means to an end.

Vaccination and public health ethics have recently come to the forefront, especially in the context of global pandemics. Christian ethics endorse the communal responsibility to protect vulnerable populations, advocating for vaccination as a means to safeguard public health. This perspective emphasizes the principle of love for one's neighbor, balancing individual freedoms with collective responsibility. Ethical considerations in public health must navigate the tension between personal autonomy and the common good, guided by a commitment to justice and compassion.

The contributions of Christian bioethicists such as Paul Ramsey and Gilbert Meilaender have significantly shaped this discourse. Ramsey's seminal work, *The Patient as Person*, foregrounded the importance of treating patients with dignity and respect, influencing debates on medical ethics and patient care. Meilaender, through his influential writings and service on the President's Council on Bioethics, has provided a robust Christian framework for addressing contemporary bioethical issues, emphasizing the moral and theological dimensions of these debates. Organizations like the Center for Bioethics and Human Dignity have furthered this work, offering resources and forums for discussion that integrate faith with bioethical inquiry.

Navigating bioethical decisions can be daunting, but Christians are not without guidance. Consulting faith-based bioethics resources provides a wealth of knowledge and insight grounded in Christian principles. Participating in bioethics discussions within church groups fosters a communal approach to these complex issues, allowing for collective wisdom and support. Engaging with medical professionals who respect Christian values ensures that medical decisions align with one's faith, providing a coherent and compassionate approach to health care. When faced with bioethical dilemmas, Christians are encouraged to seek wisdom through prayer, study, and community, trusting that their faith will illuminate the path forward.

ADDRESSING ECONOMIC INEQUALITY THROUGH CHRISTIAN TEACHINGS

Consider the ancient laws of gleaning and the Year of Jubilee, mandates found in the Old Testament that underscore the importance of economic justice and compassion for the poor. In Leviticus 19:9-10, the Israelites are instructed not to reap to the very edges of their fields or gather the gleanings of their harvest but to leave them for the poor and the foreigner. This practice ensured that the marginalized had access to food and sustenance, reflecting a divine concern for the welfare of all. Similarly, the Year of Jubilee, described in Leviticus 25, called for the periodic redistribution of land and the release of debts, aiming to prevent the entrenchment of poverty and the accumulation of wealth by a few. These laws, steeped in the theology of justice, reveal a divine blueprint for a society where resources are shared equitably and the dignity of every individual is upheld.

Jesus' teachings further amplify this call for economic justice. In the parable of the rich man and Lazarus (Luke 16:19-31), Jesus starkly contrasts the lives of the wealthy and the impoverished, warning of the spiritual peril of ignoring the needs of the poor. His admonition to the rich young ruler to sell all he has and give to the poor (Matthew 19:21) underscores the principle that true discipleship involves radical generosity and a commitment to economic equity.

The early Church, as depicted in Acts 2:44-45, practiced communal sharing, where believers "had everything in common" and "sold property and possessions to give to anyone who had need." This model of communal living underscores the Christian imperative to address economic disparity through collective action and mutual support.

Modern economic inequality, viewed through a Christian lens, presents a myriad of challenges that demand thoughtful and principled responses. Wage disparity remains a pressing issue, where the gap between executive compensation and the wages of average workers has widened dramatically. Christian ethics call for fair labor practices that ensure just wages and humane working conditions, emphasizing the inherent dignity of all labor. Access to education and healthcare, fundamental to human flourishing, is often limited by economic status, exacerbating social inequities. From a Christian perspective, addressing these disparities involves advocating for policies that provide equitable access to these vital resources, recognizing them as essential to the well-being of individuals and communities.

The impact of globalization on economic justice further complicates the landscape. While globalization has lifted many out of poverty, it has also led to the exploitation of labor and the concentration of wealth in the hands of a few. Christian teachings urge a response that prioritizes the common good over individual gain, advocating for fair trade practices and ethical sourcing that ensure workers' rights are protected and that economic benefits are distributed more equitably. The global reach of commerce demands a moral framework that transcends national boundaries, reflecting the universal scope of Christian ethics.

Christian organizations play a pivotal role in addressing economic inequality through various initiatives and programs. Church-based food banks and shelters provide immediate relief to those in need, embodying the Christian call to feed the hungry and shelter the homeless. Microfinance programs, supported by Christian charities, empower individuals in impoverished communities by providing access to small loans that enable them to start businesses and improve their livelihoods. Advocacy for fair trade and ethical sourcing ensures that the products we consume are made under fair labor conditions, promoting economic justice on a global scale.

For Christians seeking to reduce economic inequality, practical steps can make a significant impact. Volunteering with faith-based social services, such as food banks and shelters, directly aids those in need and fosters a spirit of compassion and solidarity. Supporting policies that promote economic justice, such as living wage laws and equitable tax policies, aligns public policy with Christian principles of fairness and equity. Practicing personal financial stewardship, in line with Christian teachings, involves using one's resources wisely and generously, prioritizing giving and ethical spending.

Reflect on the ways you can contribute to addressing economic inequality in your own life and community. Consider the biblical principles of justice and generosity that underpin your faith, and seek opportunities to embody these values through your actions and advocacy. Engage with your church and broader community to support initiatives that promote economic justice, and strive to create a society that reflects the compassionate and equitable vision of the Kingdom of God.

ENVIRONMENTAL STEWARDSHIP: A CHRISTIAN RESPONSIBILITY

The biblical basis for environmental stewardship is deeply rooted in the Scriptures, offering a compelling mandate for Christians to care for creation. In the Genesis narrative, God commands humanity to "fill the earth and subdue it" and to "have dominion over the fish of the sea, the birds of the air, and every living thing that moves upon the earth" (Genesis 1:28). This dominion, however, is not a license for exploitation but a call to stewardship, a sacred trust to manage and protect the natural world. The Psalms and Proverbs further elaborate on the beauty and value of nature, extolling the majesty of God's creation. "The earth is the Lord's and the fullness thereof," declares Psalm 24:1, reminding us that the world belongs to God and we are its caretakers. Proverbs 12:10 emphasizes the righteous treatment of animals, underscoring the ethical responsibility to care for all living creatures. The New Testament also reinforces this stewardship ethic, with passages like Romans 8:19-23 depicting creation groaning for redemption, highlighting the interconnectedness of human and environmental well-being.

Contemporary environmental issues present significant challenges that require a Christian perspective for thoughtful engagement. Climate change and global warming are perhaps the most pressing concerns, with rising temperatures and extreme weather events threatening ecosystems and human communities alike. From a Christian viewpoint, addressing climate change involves recognizing the moral imperative to reduce carbon emissions and mitigate environmental harm, reflecting the biblical call to love one's neighbor by protecting the planet for future generations. Conservation of biodiversity is another critical issue, as the loss of species and habitats disrupts the ecological balance and diminishes the richness of God's creation. Christians are called to advocate for policies and practices that preserve biodiversity, ensuring the health and sustainability of ecosystems.

Sustainable agriculture and food security are also paramount concerns, particularly as the global population continues to grow. Christian ethics emphasize the importance of feeding the hungry and ensuring that agricultural practices do not exploit the land or harm vulnerable communities. This involves promoting sustainable farming techniques that maintain soil fertility, conserve water, and reduce the use of harmful chemicals. Pollution and waste management present additional ethical challenges, as the accumulation of plastic waste, toxic pollutants, and other contaminants degrades the environment and poses health risks. Christians are urged to adopt and support measures that reduce waste, recycle materials, and prevent pollution, aligning with the biblical mandate to care for creation.

Christian environmental organizations play a pivotal role in addressing these issues and mobilizing faith communities for action. The Evangelical Environmental Network (EEN), for instance, has been at the forefront of advocating for climate action, emphasizing the moral and theological reasons for caring for the environment. EEN's initiatives include campaigns to reduce carbon emissions, protect vulnerable populations from environmental hazards, and promote renewable energy. A Rocha, an international Christian conservation organization, engages in hands-on conservation projects, scientific research, and environmental education. Their work in habitat restoration, species protection, and community-based conservation exemplifies how Christian principles can be applied to environmental stewardship. The Green Bible, which highlights passages related to creation care, has also influenced eco-theology, encouraging Christians to see environmental stewardship as an integral part of their faith.

For Christians committed to environmental stewardship, practical steps can make a significant difference in daily life. Reducing one's carbon footprint through lifestyle changes, such as using energy-efficient appliances, driving less, and conserving water, reflects a commitment to sustainability. Supporting sustainable products and companies that prioritize ethical and eco-friendly practices aligns consumer choices with Christian values. Participating in church-led environmental initiatives, like community clean-up events, tree planting, and advocacy for environmental policies, fosters a collective approach to stewardship and amplifies the impact of individual actions.

Reflect on how your daily practices, consumer choices, and community involvement can embody the biblical call to care for creation. Consider the interconnectedness of all creation and the responsibility to protect the environment for future generations, and seek ways to integrate these principles into your life and faith community.

FAITH-BASED RESPONSES TO SOCIAL INJUSTICE

The biblical call to address social injustice is unequivocal, resonating through the annals of Scripture with a clarion call for justice and righteousness. The Old Testament prophets, such as Isaiah, Amos, and Micah, fervently decried the injustices of their times, condemning the exploitation of the poor, the corruption of leaders, and the oppression of the marginalized. Isaiah 1:17, for instance, implores, "Learn to do good; seek justice, correct oppression; bring justice to the fatherless, plead the widow's cause." These prophetic voices echo through the ages, urging contemporary Christians to confront the systemic injustices that persist in our world.

Jesus' mission to the marginalized and oppressed is a cornerstone of the Christian faith, embodying a radical inclusivity and compassion that transcends social barriers. His ministry was marked by a profound engagement with those on the peripheries of society—the poor, the sick, the outcasts, and the sinners. In Luke 4:18-19, Jesus declares His mission: "The Spirit of the Lord is upon me, because he has anointed me to proclaim good news to the poor. He has sent me to proclaim liberty to the captives and recovery of sight to the blind, to set at liberty those who are oppressed, to proclaim the year of the Lord's favor." This proclamation underscores the imperative for Christians to follow in His footsteps, advocating for the rights and dignity of all people.

The New Testament teachings on equity and fairness further elucidate the Christian responsibility to address social injustice. The Apostle James admonishes believers to show no partiality, warning against favoritism towards the wealthy and discrimination against the poor (James 2:1-9). Paul's epistles, too, emphasize the unity and equality of all believers in Christ, breaking down the social hierarchies of Jew and Gentile, slave and free, male and female (Galatians 3:28). These teachings challenge contemporary Christians to dismantle the structures of inequality and to foster communities rooted in justice and mutual respect.

When examining specific social injustices through a Christian lens, the principles of justice and righteousness provide a robust framework for critique and action. Racial inequality and systemic racism remain pervasive issues, manifesting in disparities in education, employment, housing, and criminal justice. The Christian response must be one of active anti-racism, seeking to dismantle the systemic barriers that perpetuate racial injustice and promote reconciliation and healing.

Gender inequality and discrimination also demand a Christian response that affirms the inherent dignity and worth of all individuals, regardless of gender. This involves challenging the patriarchal structures that marginalize women and advocating for equal opportunities and rights in all spheres of life. Human trafficking and modern slavery, which exploit the most vulnerable for labor and sexual exploitation, are egregious violations of human dignity. Christians are called to combat these heinous practices through advocacy, support for survivors, and efforts to disrupt the networks that perpetuate trafficking.

The plight of refugees and immigrants, often fleeing violence, persecution, and poverty, is another urgent area of concern. The biblical mandate to "love the stranger" (Deuteronomy 10:19) compels Christians to advocate for humane immigration policies, to provide sanctuary and support for refugees, and to work towards a more just and compassionate world.

Christian organizations play a pivotal role in combating social injustice through various initiatives and programs. The International Justice Mission (IJM), for example, is at the forefront of anti-trafficking efforts, rescuing victims, bringing perpetrators to justice, and supporting survivors in their recovery. The role of the church in the Civil Rights Movement, exemplified by leaders like Dr. Martin Luther King Jr., underscores the power of faith-based advocacy for racial justice and equality. Faith-based advocacy for immigration reform, championed by organizations like the Evangelical Immigration Table, highlights the ongoing commitment to justice for immigrants and refugees.

For Christians engaged in social justice work, practical steps can amplify their impact. Volunteering with justice-focused organizations, whether through local community groups or international

NGOs, provides direct support to those in need and fosters a spirit of solidarity and compassion. Advocating for policy changes that promote equality, such as criminal justice reform, gender equality legislation, and fair immigration policies, leverages the power of collective action to effect systemic change. Educating oneself and others on issues of justice and advocacy, through workshops, reading groups, and public forums, enhances awareness and equips individuals to engage more effectively in social justice work.

Reflect on how you can embody the biblical call to justice in your own life, and consider the ways in which your faith community can collectively address social injustices. Engage with organizations and initiatives that align with your values, and seek to educate and advocate for a more just and equitable world.

THE FUTURE OF CHRISTIANITY IN AMERICA

In the stillness of a dimly lit room, a young woman kneels before her laptop, participating in a virtual prayer group. Her screen flickers with the faces of fellow believers, each in their own corner of the world, united in a digital communion that transcends physical boundaries. This image, once the stuff of science fiction, is now a reality for millions. As we stand on the precipice of a new era, it becomes evident that technology is not merely an adjunct to religious life but a transformative force reshaping the very essence of faith and community.

THE ROLE OF TECHNOLOGY IN THE FUTURE OF FAITH

The advent of technology has irrevocably altered the landscape of religious experiences, ushering in an era where faith can be practiced and nurtured through digital means. Online church services and virtual worship experiences have become commonplace, especially in the wake of the COVID-19 pandemic. These virtual gatherings, facilitated by platforms like Zoom and YouTube, have allowed congregations to maintain a sense of community and spiritual connection even when physical gatherings were impossible. The ability to stream services live, replay sermons, and engage in real-time chat discussions has democratized access to spiritual nourishment, breaking down geographical barriers and reaching individuals who might otherwise be isolated.

Similarly, the proliferation of apps for Bible study and prayer groups has revolutionized personal and communal religious practices. Apps like YouVersion and BibleGateway offer users a plethora of resources, from daily devotionals to in-depth Bible study plans, all accessible with a few taps on a smartphone. These digital tools enable believers to engage with scripture and prayer on the go, integrating faith seamlessly into their daily routines. Virtual reality (VR) experiences, though still in their nascent stages, hold the potential to provide immersive spiritual encounters. Imagine donning a VR headset and finding oneself in a meticulously recreated ancient Jerusalem, walking the paths Jesus once trod, or attending a virtual pilgrimage to the Vatican. Such experiences can deepen one's spiritual engagement, offering a visceral connection to historical and sacred sites.

While the benefits of digital faith practices are manifold, they are not without challenges. The increased accessibility afforded by technology is undoubtedly a boon for remote or disabled individuals who may find attending physical services difficult. However, this convenience comes at a cost. The potential for reduced personal interaction and community bonding is a significant drawback. The tactile, face-to-face connections that form the bedrock of many religious communities cannot be fully replicated in a digital environment. Additionally, security concerns related to digital data and privacy present a formidable challenge. As more religious activities move online, the risk of data breaches and unauthorized access to personal information grows. Ensuring the security of digital platforms must be a priority for religious organizations to maintain trust and protect their congregants.

Innovative uses of technology by religious organizations demonstrate the potential for digital tools to enhance ministry and outreach. Social media platforms like Facebook, Instagram, and Twitter have become vital channels for evangelism and community engagement. Churches and religious groups utilize these platforms to share inspirational content, announce events, and foster discussions, reaching a global audience. Live-streaming of religious events and conferences has also gained traction, allowing individuals worldwide to participate in significant religious gatherings from the comfort of their homes. Interactive online platforms for theological education, such as Coursera and edX, offer courses on religious studies, enabling believers to deepen their understanding of theology and scripture from esteemed institutions.

As we look to the future, several technological advancements promise to further transform religious experiences. Artificial intelligence (AI) holds significant potential for personalized spiritual guidance. AI-driven chatbots and virtual assistants could provide tailored spiritual advice, recommend scripture passages, and offer prayer support, enhancing the accessibility and personalization of religious experiences. Blockchain technology, known for its security and transparency, could revolutionize donation tracking, ensuring that contributions are securely recorded and transparently allocated. This could enhance trust in religious organizations and encourage more generous giving. Augmented reality (AR) offers another exciting frontier, potentially providing immersive scripture-reading experiences. Imagine using an AR app to visualize biblical scenes while reading scripture, adding a layer of depth and engagement to the reading experience.

The intersection of technology and faith presents both opportunities and challenges, requiring thoughtful navigation to harness the benefits while mitigating the drawbacks. As technology continues to evolve, so too will its impact on religious practices, shaping the future of Christianity in ways we are only beginning to comprehend. For believers, religious leaders, and theologians alike, embracing these technological advancements with discernment and wisdom will be crucial in ensuring that the essence of faith remains intact in this digital age.

Reflection Section: Engaging with Digital Faith

1. **Assess Your Digital Faith Practices**:
   - Reflect on how you currently use technology to enhance your spiritual life. Do you participate in online worship services, use Bible study apps, or engage in virtual prayer groups? How have these practices enriched your faith?

2. **Identify Potential Challenges**:
   - Consider the challenges you face in engaging with digital faith practices. Do you find it difficult to connect with others online? Are you concerned about the security of your personal information? How can you address these challenges to improve your digital faith experience?

3. **Explore New Technological Tools**:
   - Research and explore new technological tools that can enhance your spiritual journey. Look into AI-driven spiritual guides, AR scripture-reading apps, and secure donation platforms. How can these tools help you deepen your faith and connect with your religious community in meaningful ways?

By reflecting on these questions, you can gain a deeper under-standing of how technology can be integrated into your spiritual life, enriching your faith while navigating the challenges that come with digital practices.

REVIVING CHRISTIAN VALUES IN EDUCATION AND GOVERNANCE

In the hallowed halls of academia, where knowledge and virtue should ideally converge, there lies an untapped potential for reintro-ducing Christian values that have historically shaped moral and ethical frameworks. The development of faith-based curricula, meticulously designed for both public and private schools, could serve as a cornerstone for this revival. By integrating biblical princi-ples into subjects such as history, literature, and even science, educators can offer students a holistic education that not only fosters intellectual growth but also moral discernment. Imagine a history lesson that not only chronicles events but also delves into the ethical implications of those events through a Christian lens or a literature class that explores the moral complexities of human nature as depicted in biblical narratives.

Partnerships between religious organizations and educational insti-tutions could further bolster this initiative. Faith-based organiza-tions, with their rich resources and expertise, can collaborate with schools to develop comprehensive curricula that are both academi-cally rigorous and spiritually enriching. These partnerships can extend beyond curriculum development to include extracurricular activities, such as faith-based service projects, mentorship programs, and spiritual retreats, all designed to cultivate a sense of community and spiritual growth among students. Advocacy for policies that allow for religious expression in schools is also crucial. This involves not only protecting the rights of students to pray and wear religious symbols but also advocating for the inclusion of voluntary faith-based activities within the school environment. By creating an atmosphere where faith is respected and integrated into the educational experience, schools can nurture well-rounded individuals who are equipped to navigate the complexities of the modern world with a strong moral compass.

Christian educators imbued with a sense of divine purpose, play a pivotal role in shaping future generations. Their influence extends beyond the confines of the classroom, as they serve as role models of integrity, compassion, and faith. Stories of Christian educators making a difference in their communities abound, from the teacher who integrates biblical principles into their pedagogy, fostering a classroom environment rooted in respect and empathy, to the principal who champions faith-based initiatives that engage and inspire students. Christian colleges and universities, with their commitment to integrating faith and learning, also exert a significant influence on public education. These institutions produce graduates who are academically proficient and deeply rooted in their faith, prepared to bring a Christian perspective to their professional and personal lives. The influence of these educators and institutions is profound, as they help shape a generation of leaders guided by Christian values in their decision-making processes.

The potential for Christian values to influence governance is equally compelling. Advocacy for laws and policies that reflect Christian ethics can lead to a more just and compassionate society. Faith-based lobbying groups, such as the Family Research Council and the Ethics & Religious Liberty Commission, play a crucial role in shaping legislation that aligns with biblical principles. These organizations advocate for policies that protect the sanctity of life, promote family values, and ensure religious freedom. Their efforts are complemented by the work of Christian politicians who bring their faith to bear on their legislative responsibilities. Examples of such politicians include former President Jimmy Carter, known for his humanitarian efforts and commitment to social justice, and Senator Tim Scott, whose faith informs his advocacy for economic opportunity and education reform. These leaders demonstrate that Christian values can inform governance in ways that promote the common good and uphold the dignity of all individuals.

Navigating the balance between church and state presents both challenges and opportunities for reviving Christian values in public life. While essential for protecting religious freedom, the principle of separation of church and state can also create obstacles for those seeking to integrate faith into public institutions. Building coalitions with like-minded organizations, both religious and secular, can help to advance common goals and overcome these obstacles. Such coalitions can advocate for policies that respect the role of faith in public life while ensuring that no single religious perspective dominates the public sphere. Addressing public skepticism and opposition is another critical challenge. In a society that is increasingly secular and diverse, efforts to reintroduce Christian values in education and governance may be met with resistance. Engaging in open and respectful dialogue, grounded in a deep understanding of both faith and reason, can help to bridge this divide. By demonstrating the positive impact of Christian values on society, advocates can build a compelling case for their integration into public life.

The potential for reintroducing Christian values in education and governance is vast, offering a pathway to a more morally and ethically grounded society. Through the development of faith-based curricula, partnerships between religious organizations and educational institutions, and advocacy for policies that allow for religious expression, schools can become nurturing grounds for both intellectual and spiritual growth. Christian educators and institutions play a crucial role in this endeavor, shaping future generations with their commitment to integrating faith and learning. In the realm of governance, faith-based principles can inform political decision-making, leading to laws and policies that promote justice, compassion, and the common good. By navigating the balance between church and state, building coalitions, and addressing public skepticism, the revival of Christian values in public life can become a reality. The journey ahead is fraught with challenges, yet the potential rewards — a society anchored in moral and ethical integrity—are immeasurable.

THE FUTURE OF CHRISTIAN INFLUENCE IN CORPORATE AMERICA

The evolving role of faith in the workplace is a subject of growing importance, given the increasing recognition that Christian principles can profoundly shape corporate culture. Initiatives aimed at creating faith-friendly workplaces are emerging across various industries, reflecting a broader trend towards inclusivity and holistic employee well-being. These initiatives often encompass policies that allow for religious expression, such as designated prayer rooms, flexible scheduling to accommodate religious observances, and faith-based employee resource groups (ERGs). Companies like Tyson Foods and American Airlines have pioneered these practices, demonstrating that when employees are permitted to bring their whole selves to work—including their faith—they exhibit higher levels of engagement, morale, and productivity.

Encouraging ethical business practices rooted in Christian values is another crucial aspect of this evolving landscape. At its core, Christianity advocates for honesty, integrity, and fairness—principles that, when applied to business, can transform corporate ethics. For instance, companies that prioritize transparency in their operations and communications, as guided by biblical teachings, often find themselves earning the trust and loyalty of both employees and customers. Ethical decision-making processes that consider the welfare of all stakeholders rather than focusing solely on profit maximization create a sustainable business model that aligns with Christian stewardship. The case of Chick-fil-A, a company that integrates faith and business by closing on Sundays and emphasizing community philanthropy, illustrates the tangible benefits of such an approach. Despite facing criticism for its stance on various social issues, Chick-fil-A remains a highly successful enterprise, suggesting that ethical consistency and community investment resonate with a significant consumer base.

The impact of Christian leadership on corporate ethics cannot be overstated. Prominent Christian CEOs, such as Truett Cathy of Chick-fil-A and Dan T. Cathy of Interstate Batteries, exemplify how faith can drive ethical change within organizations. These leaders are known for their servant leadership style, which prioritizes the needs of employees, customers, and the broader community over personal gain. This approach fosters a corporate culture of empathy, humility, and service, which not only enhances internal morale but also builds a positive public image. Success stories of ethical decision-making in challenging situations further highlight the influence of Christian leadership. For example, during the 2008 financial crisis, some Christian-led businesses chose to retain employees and invest in their communities, even at the expense of short-term profits. These decisions, grounded in Christian ethics, ultimately contributed to long-term resilience and success, reinforcing the idea that ethical leadership is not only morally right but also strategically sound.

The potential for faith-based corporate social responsibility (CSR) to shape the future of business is immense. Christian values can guide CSR initiatives in various impactful ways, from environmental sustainability to corporate philanthropy. Faith-driven approaches to environmental sustainability, for instance, emphasize the biblical mandate of stewardship over creation. Companies like Patagonia, while not explicitly Christian, exemplify this principle by committing to environmental conservation and sustainable business practices. Corporate philanthropy inspired by Christian teachings often involves not just financial donations but also active participation in community service projects. Businesses that encourage employees to volunteer and engage with local communities embody the Christian principle of loving one's neighbor, creating a ripple effect of positive change. Community engagement initiatives, such as sponsoring local events, supporting educational programs, and providing disaster relief, further illustrate how businesses can live out their faith through actions that benefit society at large.

Looking ahead, several trends suggest that Christian values will continue to influence corporate America in meaningful ways. There is an increasing demand for transparency and ethical practices, driven by both consumer expectations and regulatory pressures. Businesses that adhere to Christian principles of honesty and integrity are well-positioned to meet these demands, fostering trust and loyalty among stakeholders. The growing importance of employee well-being and spiritual care is another significant trend. Companies are beginning to recognize that addressing the spiritual needs of employees can lead to enhanced job satisfaction, reduced turnover, and improved overall well-being. Initiatives such as providing access to chaplaincy services, offering faith-based wellness programs, and creating supportive environments for religious expression reflect this understanding.

Collaboration between faith-based and secular organizations for common goals is also on the rise. These partnerships can address a wide range of societal issues, from poverty alleviation to environmental sustainability, by leveraging the strengths and resources of both sectors. For example, faith-based organizations might bring a deep commitment to service and moral integrity, while secular organizations contribute technical expertise and broader reach. Such collaborations can create synergies that amplify the impact of CSR initiatives, demonstrating that faith and reason can work together to achieve the common good.

As we move forward, integrating Christian values into corporate America offers a pathway to a more ethical, compassionate, and sustainable business environment. By fostering faith-friendly workplaces, encouraging ethical business practices, and leveraging the influence of Christian leadership, companies can create cultures that not only thrive economically but also contribute positively to society. The trends of increased transparency, focus on employee well-being, and collaborative efforts between faith-based and secular entities further underscore the relevance of Christian principles in shaping the future of business. This integration promises not only to enhance corporate ethics but also to reaffirm the role of faith in addressing the complex challenges of our modern world.

CONCLUSION

As we reach the denouement of our exploration into the shifting sands of faith within the fabric of American society, it is imperative to distill the essence of our journey. From the hallowed halls of independence to the bustling modern classrooms, corporate boardrooms, and the intricate corridors of government, we have meticulously examined the erosion of Christian influence and the ramifications thereof.

Our odyssey began with the historical foundations of faith in America, tracing the indelible mark Christianity has left on the nation's founding documents and early governance. We delved into the symbiotic relationship between church and state, the moral imperatives that shaped early legal frameworks, and the profound role of religious education in molding the minds of citizens. This historical context provided a poignant contrast to the contemporary secularization of public schools, the gradual excision of prayer and Bible reading, and the rise of secular moral education, all of which underscore a significant paradigmatic shift.

In the realm of governance, we scrutinized the diminishing presence of religious rhetoric in political discourse and the judiciary's pivotal role in enforcing secular principles. We reflected on the policy changes that have systematically marginalized religious expression, revealing the complex interplay between religion and state in modern America.

Turning our gaze to corporate America, we observed the metamorphosis from Christian ethics to a secular corporate ethos. This shift has manifested in the rise of corporate social responsibility with a secular focus, as well as the challenges faced by faith-based employee resource groups in maintaining religious expression within a predominantly secular workspace. We examined case studies of corporations that have either embraced or distanced themselves from Christian values, offering a nuanced perspective on the ethical landscape of modern business.

The consequences of secularization were laid bare as we analyzed the erosion of moral and ethical standards, the rise of secular humanism, and the impact on mental health and spiritual well-being. The decline of religion's influence on community and social cohesion was juxtaposed with successful secular initiatives, highlighting the potential for building inclusive communities despite the waning presence of traditional religious institutions.

We ventured into the realm of interfaith dialogue, emphasizing its critical role in fostering mutual respect, preventing religious extremism, and enhancing community development. The shared ethical and moral principles among major religions were underscored, offering a hopeful vision for collaborative efforts in addressing contemporary social issues.

In addressing modern ethical and moral dilemmas, we drew upon Christian teachings to navigate bioethical issues, economic inequality, environmental stewardship, and social injustice. These applications of faith in contemporary contexts illustrated the timeless relevance of Christian principles in guiding ethical decision-making and fostering a just society.

As we contemplate the future of Christianity in America, the transformative role of technology stands out as a beacon of hope and challenge. Digital faith practices, online worship, and the integration of advanced technologies such as AI and VR present unprecedented opportunities for spiritual growth and community building, albeit with inherent challenges that must be navigated with discernment and integrity.

The historical roots of Christianity in America have been profoundly influential, yet the contemporary landscape is marked by a pronounced secularization that challenges traditional religious paradigms. Despite this, the enduring principles of Christian ethics continue to offer profound guidance on issues ranging from governance and education to business and social justice. The rise of secular humanism and the decline of religious influence pose significant challenges, yet the potential for interfaith dialogue and technological innovation offers avenues for reinvigorating faith in modern contexts.

As a person of faith who has traversed the corridors of Catholic education and corporate America, I implore you to reflect on the insights garnered from this exploration and consider the role you can play in fostering a society that upholds ethical principles and spiritual integrity. Whether through engaging in interfaith dialogue, advocating for faith-informed policies, or integrating Christian ethics into your professional and personal life, your actions have the potential to shape the moral and spiritual fabric of our society.

In conclusion, the journey we have undertaken is not merely an academic exercise but a call to action. It is a summons to reaffirm the values that have historically underpinned our society and to navigate the complexities of modern life with a steadfast commitment to faith and ethics. As we stand at the crossroads of tradition and modernity, let us endeavor to create a future where faith and reason coexist harmoniously, guiding us toward a more just, compassionate, and spiritually enriched society.

BIBLIOGRAPHY

God in the Declaration of Independence https://wifamilycouncil.org/radio/god-in-the-declaration-of-independence/

Northwest Ordinance (1787) https://www.archives.gov/milestone-documents/northwest-ordinance

George Washington's Farewell Address https://virginiahistory.org/learn/george-washingtons-farewell-address

Introduction: Christianity and American Law https://www.cambridge.org/core/books/great-christian-jurists-in-american-history/introduction-christianity-and-american-law/5AEA44725A0B80CCAD5DDD2252D8148E

Horace Mann | The First Amendment Encyclopedia https://firstamendment.mtsu.edu/article/horace-mann/

Illinois ex rel. McCollum v. Board of Ed. of School Dist. No. ... https://www.oyez.org/cases/1940-1955/333us203

John Dewey | Biography, Philosophy, Pragmatism, & ... https://www.britannica.com/biography/John-Dewey

Facts and Case Summary - Engel v. Vitale https://www.uscourts.gov/educational-resources/educational-activities/facts-and-case-summary-engel-v-vitale

Religious Rhetoric and American Politics - Project MUSE https://muse.jhu.edu/book/24104/

The Supreme Court Benches the Separation of Church and ... https://www.aclu.org/news/religious-liberty/the-supreme-court-benches-the-separation-of-church-and-state

Religious Liberty Should Do No Harm https://www.americanprogress.org/article/religious-liberty-no-harm/

Modeling the Future of Religion in America https://www.pewresearch.org/religion/2022/09/13/modeling-the-future-of-religion-in-america/

A History of Business Ethics https://www.scu.edu/ethics/focus-areas/business-ethics/resources/a-history-of-business-ethics/

The Debate over the Shareholder Model of Corporate ... https://harbert.auburn.edu/binaries/documents/center-for-ethical-organizational-cultures/debate_issues/shareholder-model.pdf

Companies Embrace Religion as New Facet of Diversity ... https://news.bloomberglaw.com/daily-labor-report/companies-embrace-religion-as-latest-facet-of-diversity-efforts

Chick-fil-A: Selling Chicken With a Side of God https://www.theatlantic.com/business/archive/2014/09/chick-fil-a-selling-chicken-with-a-side-of-god/379776/

Secularity's Influence on the Moral Compass of Society https://www.integrative-psych.org/resources/secularitys-influence-on-the-moral-compass-of-society-navigating-values-in-a-changing-world.

We Cannot Separate Christian Morals and the Rule of Law https://imprimis.hillsdale.edu/we-cannot-separate-christian-morals-and-the-rule-of-law/

Secular Humanism Defined https://secularhumanism.org/what-is-secular-humanism/secular-humanism-defined/

Religion and mental health - PMC https://www.ncbi.nlm.nih.gov/pmc/articles/PMC3705681/

The Importance of Interfaith Dialogue - Religion & Peace https://blog.hartfordinternational.edu/2024/05/23/importance-of-interfaith-dialogue/

Interfaith Programs on College Campuses: Lessons Learned https://www.start.umd.edu/sites/default/files/publications/local_attachments/20110425_Wilkenfeld_InterfaithProgramsonCampuses.pdf

Do Buddhism and Christianity have common ground in ethics? https://carm.org/buddhism/do-buddhism-and-christianity-have-common-ground-in-ethics/

Media Portrayals of Religion: Christianity | MediaSmarts https://mediasmarts.ca/diversity-media/religion/media-portrayals-religion-christianity.

Christian Ethics https://www.thegospelcoalition.org/essay/christian-ethics/

How to Apply Christian Ethics to Business Practices https://www.bluefield.edu/blog/importance-christian-ethics-business/

Social Movements and Religion in American History https://www.thearda.com/us-religion/history/timelines/interactive-display?tid=2

Faith in the workplace: Integrating spirituality and career https://blogs.crossmap.com/stories/faith-in-the-workplace-integrating-spirituality-and-career-dvRXnxJxg-faqTQEPBkI9

Doubt & Faith: Top Reasons People Question Christianity https://www.barna.com/research/doubt-faith/

The Doubting Process: A Longitudinal Study ... https://www.ncbi.nlm.nih.gov/pmc/articles/PMC2839364/

St. Thomas Aquinas on faith and doubt | Petty Armchair Popery https://agellius.wordpress.com/2012/10/30/st-thomas-aquinas-on-faith-and-doubt/

10 Spiritual Disciplines to Strengthen Your Faith https://www.cru.org/us/en/train-and-grow/spiritual-growth/spiritual-disciplines-strengthen-faith.html

34 Ethical Issues All Christians Should Know https://www.crossway.org/articles/34-ethical-issues-all-christians-should-know/

Applying Church Teachings in the Process of Making Moral ... https://www.smp.org/dynamicmedia/files/b6398e335d5ee93fa1cac2e4e039018e/TX001531_1-

Background-Applying_Church_Teachings_in_the_Process_of_Making_ Moral_Decisions.pdf

Bioethicist: Christians must make argument for 'particular ... https://cruxnow.com/ interviews/2020/07/bioethicist-christians-must-make-argument-for-particular- moral-vision/

Five Things Christians Should Know about Income Inequality https://tifwe.org/five- ideas-christians-should-know-about-income-inequality/

Use of apps and websites in religious life https://www.pewresearch.org/religion/ 2023/06/02/use-of-apps-and-websites-in-religious-life/

Religion in the Public Schools https://www.pewresearch.org/religion/2019/10/03/reli gion-in-the-public-schools-2019-update/

Christian Businesses and Ethical Leadership - Convene https://www.convenenow. com/blog/ethical-leadership-how-christian-businesses-are-changing-the-business- world

Becoming a Faith-Friendly Workplace | RFBF https://religiousfreedomandbusiness. org/becoming-a-faith-friendly-workplace

* 9 7 9 8 3 3 0 6 4 4 5 8 2 *